# HARD CHOICES

Policy autonomy and priority-setting
in public expenditure

Eastern Health and Social Services Board

Democratic Dialogue (report 10)
Eastern Health & Social Services Board
Northern Ireland Economic Council
(occasional paper 10)
December 1998

Further copies available from:

Democratic Dialogue
53 University Street
Belfast BT7 1FY
Tel: 01232-232228/232230/232525
Fax: 01232-233334
E-mail: dd@dem-dial.demon.co.uk
Web site: www.dem-dial.demon.co.uk

Eastern Health & Social Services Board
Champion House
12-22 Linenhall Street
Belfast BT2 8BS
Tel: 01232-321313
E-mail: Enquiry@ehssb.n-i.nhs.uk

Northern Ireland Economic Council
Bulloch House
2 Linenhall Street
Belfast BT2 8BA
Tel: 01232-232125
Fax: 01232-331250

©DD/EHSSB/NIEC 1998
ISBN 1 900281 09 0

Cover design by Dunbar Design
Photographs by Lesley Doyle
Printed by Regency Press

**Democratic Dialogue** was established in 1995 to promote new thinking about Northern Ireland—political, economic, social and cultural. It has worked in a participatory mode, using round-tables, citizens' juries, focus groups and so on. It also organises lectures and seminars to further debate. It works in partnership with other organisations on projects, and seeks to secure not only publicity for the results but also policy impact. It is connected to a range of Irish, British and international policy networks. Details of its publications are appended to this report.

**The Eastern Health and Social Services Board** is a non-departmental body assessing need and commissioning health and personal social services for 660,000 people, as well as monitoring services and assessing health outcomes and promoting health and social well-being. It has an annual budget of almost £500 million. The board has developed expertise in resource allocation and prioritisation of service development, to ensure resources are equitably distributed. Redistribution can be contentious and has required the board to develop objective approaches which it can share with the public and its representatives.

**The Northern Ireland Economic Council** is an advisory body set up by the secretary of state in 1977. It is a successful example of consensual social partnership, comprising representatives of business, trade unions and independents. It has a wide remit to provide independent advice to the secretary of state on economic policy for Northern Ireland. It generates three series of publications: reports, occasional papers and research monographs. A list of the more recent is appended. In addition, the council holds seminars and conferences, often in partnership with other organisations, to promote debate.

# Contents

| | | |
|---|---|---|
| Preface | | 4 |
| Executive summary | | 5 |
| Introduction | ROBIN WILSON | 8 |
| Autonomy is strength | JOHN LOUGHLIN | 13 |
| Bang for the buck | VANI BOROOAH | 37 |
| Public expenditure on the eve of devolution | RICHARD BARNETT<br>GRAEME HUTCHINSON | 48 |
| Fiscal opportunities | DAVID HEALD | 71 |
| Conclusion | PAUL GORECKI | 88 |
| Notes on contributors | | 95 |

# Preface

This report is the product of a unique partnership between the think tank Democratic Dialogue, the Eastern Health and Social Services Board and the Northern Ireland Economic Council.

The three organisations came together behind this project because they were concerned to see a sharper focus on the very real dilemmas issues involving public expenditure will pose for elected representatives in Northern Ireland, as and when devolution takes effect.

DD was established in 1995 partly out of concern that economic and social issues were not sufficiently debated to prepare politicians for the intense pressures of government. For its part, the EHSSB has, of necessity, daily to confront how it sets priorities within limited budgets. And the NIEC has a record of interest in the implications for the region of 'decentralised governance' (see appended publications).

The views expressed by the contributors are, of course, their own. But all three organisations would strongly welcome opportunities to continue this debate in other public formats. Details of each can be found on the inside front cover of this publication. ■

# Executive summary

Northern Ireland is on the cusp of a new era. If the post-agreement impasse over paramilitary weapons decommissioning can be broken, a wholly new climate for its elected representatives and civic leaders hoves into view.

In this complex new political architecture, the most significant element will be the replacement of the paternalism of 'direct rule' from Westminster by the democratic Assembly at Stormont and its Executive Committee. Yet the exercise of autonomy in the modern world means something quite other than what it meant in 1972 (see John Loughlin's chapter).

The post-war period has seen the progression of three paradigms of the state: the expansive welfare state (1945ff), the contracting neo-liberal state (1979ff) and what might be called the communitarian/social state. This last, emergent model, characteristic of Blairism, sustains neither the command-and-control approach of the welfare estate nor the leave-all-to-the-market stance of the neo-liberals.

It is an *enabling* state, in which the pursuit of equality of opportunity and social justice is no longer counterposed to an environment favouring competition and excellence. The new paradigm is characterised by slimmed-down bureaucracy, with devolution of power to regions and revitalised local government, and much 'governance'—the business of government—taking place through networks that include civil society.

Thus while the new Assembly chimes with international trends, its politicians will find the exercise of government by no means the pulling of the relatively simple levers of a quarter century ago. Moreover, what precise autonomy they will have is moot: as the UK is not a federal state with a written constitution, Westminster overrides may still come into play—or there may be arguments as to whether they should—especially in the field of external 'para-diplomacy'. The task is to find the right level of autonomy in addressing the challenges of globalisation and competition.

There has been growing pressure upon the public purse in recent decades, in particular with an ageing population and increasing social insecurity (see Vani Borooah's chapter). But if this has led to public-expenditure cuts and privatisation internationally, there remains a case for government intervention in the economy—the problem of market failure. Indeed, the old debate around how much governmental intervention has become a debate about its *quality*. For example, government needs to underwrite general, non-firm-specific training to overcome the fears of firms that any investment in training would be recouped by others through poaching of trained workers.

Market failure in Northern Ireland is reflected above all in the failure of the labour market to clear. Unemployment, though recently reduced and no longer the highest in the UK, remains high—especially long-term unemployment—and is surrounded by a much larger penumbra of social exclusion, exacerbated by recent trends widening inequalities between individuals and households. Social inclusion is the priority area for public expenditure and policy-making.

Since 1978, Northern Ireland's public-expenditure allocation—like that of Scotland and Wales—has been determined by the so-called Barnett formula, whereby increases in comparable programmes in Great Britain are matched in the region according to a population-based ratio (see the chapter by Barnett and Hutchinson). Yet the formula has yet to be applied in the context of decentralised government for which it was devised, owing to the collapse of the then Labour administration's devolution plans.

But devolution implies choice over priorities—not simply following central-government programmes. This in turn implies a need for marginal tax-varying powers—as in the Scotland but not the Northern Ireland bill—so that the regional administration is to some extent accountable for its decisions. If retained, the 'parity principle'—applied to social security, UK-wide salaries for public servants, agriculture, health, education and housing—will, however, greatly restrict the apparently large discretion in public-expenditure allocation devolution the Northern Ireland Assembly will enjoy.

Yet the Assembly can, and should, set itself ambitious policy targets, particularly in economic development and the quality of public decision-making. If this will pose challenges for regional politicians, used to decades in opposition, all-round UK devolution will also challenge the notion that Westminster parties campaign on UK-wide manifestoes. Central government will have to learn to 'let go'.

The dynamics of the Barnett formula and the detail of public-expenditure accounting for the territories are very complicated (see David Heald's chapter). But the increased visibility of fiscal transfers to Northern Ireland, Scotland and Wales is likely to bring pressure for reduction of the differential support they enjoy. The best response by the devolved bodies is to embrace transparency and support a comprehensive needs assessment and an Australian-style Territorial Exchequer Board.

Within Northern Ireland, better value for money should be sought via a review of the machinery of government, including, for example, the administrative arrangements for health, social services and education. Special Treasury support will be required for the up-front redundancy costs of reduced 'law and order' provision, which may mean later savings returning to the Treasury rather than being transferred to other programmes.

Greater openness in public-expenditure decision-making should be established, with the Department of Finance and Personnel required to present costed options to Assembly committees. Confusing official public-expenditure documentation should be rationalised and each of the major Assembly parties needs to designate someone who can master the specialist expertise required to engage with the civil servants involved.

The following conclusions (as Paul Gorecki elaborates) can be drawn:
- The Barnett formula institutionalised Northern Ireland's relatively favourable public-expenditure treatment. This is likely to be increasingly questioned, and some new method for allocating expenditure across the UK devised.
- For reasons of both accountability and efficiency, the Assembly should be given tax-varying powers. A regional income tax would be the best mechanism.
- Northern Ireland's political culture remains largely set in the climate of the 'expansive welfare state'. This encourages unrealistic expectations about the degree to which the state can solve the region's social and economic problems.
- The involuntary coalition which is to be the Executive Committee and the dispersal of power in the new dispensation, allied to the continued dominance of the UK system of governance, will mean change will be initially slow.
- Given the cold climate for public expenditure, the quality of public-policy decisions, priority-setting and value for money come to the fore. Growth with development should be the goal of the new administration. ■

# Introduction

**Robin Wilson**

As well as great opportunities, in the wake of the Belfast agreement Northern Ireland faces unprecedented challenges. Perhaps the most important has been least discussed: how to ensure policy autonomy is used creatively to bring tangible change to a war-weary population with otherwise largely the same aspirations for themselves and their families as anywhere else; how also to set priorities such that expectations are realistic and can be effectively met.

It was to this end that the three partners in this project jointly organised a round-table in Belfast in June, courtesy of the Eastern Health and Social Services Board, on the theme of policy autonomy and priority-setting. This publication is the result, though hopefully only the beginning of a much larger debate which, while technically difficult—in as much as it touches on complex issues of public expenditure and budgeting—is far too important to be left, in effect, to a coterie of civil servants. And this introduction seeks to give just a flavour of the range of stimulating contributions made around the table that day.

As one senior politician has put it, Northern Ireland has developed a political culture of 'protest and demand'. Richard Barnett and Graeme Hutchinson see this as attuned to decades of permanent opposition under direct rule but wholly inappropriate to the new context where almost all parties are moving from opposition to government. That means a *Gestalt* shift from the conservatism of saying no to unacceptable government plans to articulating positive policy alternatives, from the luxury of demanding new expenditure as a solution to every problem to the hard choices of working within fixed budgets, from the introversion of a 'provincial' politics to the outward-looking learning required in a fast-changing policy environment.

The biggest danger facing the Belfast agreement—apart, of course, from its collapse—is the mundane threat of bad government. Bear in mind that the agreement prevents citizens exercising what could be seen as the ultimate democratic right: to 'turf the scoundrels out'. Thus in Belgium, with its similar power-sharing arrangements, the same cast of characters has reappeared in government after successive elections—contributing to the alienation evident on the ground.[1]

One potential source of such cynicism could be continued attrition in government by unionists and nationalists—including over whether policy might or might not depart substantially from that prevalent in Great Britain, as a senior government official warned the roundtable in June. Hitherto, the 'parity principle', while ensuring welcome support via the Westminster subvention for service quality and public-sector employment, has militated against innovation except at the margin (for example, the ineffective 'targeting social need' and 'policy appraisal and fair treatment' initiatives).

As Sir George Quigley, outgoing chair of the Northern Ireland Economic Council, put it, parity was 'the God' under the old Stormont arrangements. He argued that the Assembly and Executive Committee should start with 'zero-based policy formation', as if (though there clearly are constraints) the region was independent. This, he suggested, could be an exciting 'joint venture' for the two main religious communities, conducted on an equal basis and with the Civic Forum acting as a 'fertiliser' of ideas.

Take health, for instance. For too long,

**There's a lot of paperwork in this job**

the EHSSB chair, Dan Thompson, said, debates about health policy and public expenditure had focused on high-technology projects (dear to powerful professional lobbies) and shroud-waving (resisting change in acute provision). This had militated against securing adequate investment in population-based prevention programmes and care for the vulnerable, chronically ill and disabled. Meanwhile, the health differentials between the wealthy and poor continued to widen—as illustrated by an emerging epidemic of suicide in young men, associated with unemployment and hopelessness.

Mr Thompson suggested the solution lay not in building more institutions but in working with communities to help them articulate their problems and develop services and local solutions. He commended the architects of the Belfast agreement and welcomed the opportunity offered by the new arrangements to put in place equitable, accessible and high-quality services, tailored towards eliminating poverty and social exclusion and achieving measurable improvements in health and social well-being in the region. He called for the designation of a minister of public health, to ensure wider public-health issues had cross-departmental prominence in the Assembly.

The Assembly and Executive Committee, as Barnett and Hutchinson argue, must set ambitious policy targets—particularly, as Vani Borooah indicates, in the achievement of sustainable economic development and social inclusion. These represent far more holistic approaches than the narrow reductions to the firm in the first instance and 'targeting social need' in the second have conventionally recognised. For example, there has been far too little public discussion—in terms of both objectives—of policy on education and training in Northern Ireland and the inadequacy of current arrangements to deliver a workforce that can enjoy a high-wage/high-productivity economy. Moreover, these two policy goals would be mutually reinforcing, whereas currently TSN is largely seen as at best marginal to, or at worst a drag upon, the 'real' business of economic development.

These concerns raise the wider question of the nature of governance, as John Loughlin stresses. In a changing architecture of levels of government throughout the European Union, the role of government is itself changing—away from a one-club approach relying entirely on financial levers of executive power (like assistance to firms or TSN) towards a much more sophisticated co-ordinating function among a range of governmental and non-governmental agencies and actors, in which the role of networks is key.[2]

In that sense, the problems of

Northern Ireland are more profound than those of market failure found more generally. They fundamentally stem from the cancer of sectarianism which has seeped through the tissues of the body politic, corroding trust and encouraging go-it-alone behaviour amongst individuals and groups—thereby crucially preventing the emergence of the common 'culture of commitment' so characteristic of the more successful European regions from which Northern Ireland must learn.[3]

It is in this context that the hitherto ill-defined role of the Civic Forum can be understood. If originally intended by its sponsors in the Stormont talks, the Women's Coalition, as a second chamber, the agreement gives it only an advisory role. But as such, the key business, trade-union and voluntary-sector components of the forum can do much to develop a simulacrum of social partnership within it, spurring government's developmental efforts and helping to deliver outcomes on the ground.[4]

A key function of the Assembly will be, as David Heald argues, to fill the 'democratic deficit' in Northern Ireland in exposing civil servants to scrutiny before its committees. This will require not only adequate professional assistance to the committees but also, as Heald emphasises, the accumulation of specialist knowledge by party groups and designated spokesperspons.

One thing is, however, clear: Northern Ireland is not going to receive any further public expenditure largesse. It has historically enjoyed much higher *per capita* spending than any other part of the UK,[5] it has had the benefit of the chancellor's special £315 million package in May[6] and it has done well out of Labour's Comprehensive Spending Review because of the weight of the education and health sectors in the Northern Ireland block.[7] It *may* (and should) be able to transfer resources from a diminishing 'law-and-order' budget to economic and social programmes, but the former remains 'reserved' to Westminster whereas the latter will be transferred to the Assembly, and the short-run costs (notably redundancy payments) of 'downsizing' the Royal Ulster Constabulary will be severe. Meanwhile, European Union support can only be expected to go down over time.

Thus, as Heald argues, rather than engage in 'clientelistic whingeing' about the volume of external funding, managing expenditure better should be the focus (which happens, *inter alia*, to be the best guarantor that external support will be sustained). It is a task made considerably easier if there are clear policy-priority lodestars to follow; the indiscriminate search for efficiency savings, by comparison, has long suffered from the law of diminishing returns.

But it remains tremendously difficult to divert monies from mainstream programmes. It is therefore also crucial, especially to achieve policy renewal, that relatively small amounts can be found to support innovative projects, trying out new policy approaches and feeding back experiment into the system. This is particularly true of the social-inclusion arena. Hence the case—apart from the claim of accountability—for some relationship between revenue and expenditure via tax-varying powers for the Assembly, as various contributors to the round-table strongly contended[8] and—to their credit—the Alliance Party and the Social Democratic and Labour Party have both subscribed.

As Sir George concluded the discussion at the round-table, beginning from identified objectives a 'shared vision' was required—a vision of Northern Ireland as a competitive region, marrying economic growth with social justice, private prosperity with good public services. Northern Ireland could develop policy, post-agreement, in a variety of external contexts, and the short-term task was to agree a programme for government. Employers, unions and the voluntary sector needed to become 'contractually committed' to clear goals.

Last but not least, he said the responsibility of political leadership was a big one. But given the scope for dispute in these matters, as the government official said in June, over all this hangs the imperative that the first and deputy first minister, and the Executive Committee, provide the 'glue' to hold the whole project together.

"If we don't get that right early on," he warned then, "I suspect we are in for some very choppy waters." ■

### Footnotes

[1] 'Living together, talking apart', *Guardian*, October 9th 1998

[2] 'Economic governance—international experiences', DD paper commissioned by the Confederation of British Industry Northern Ireland, Belfast, March 1998

[3] *Successful European Regions: Northern Ireland Learning from Others*, Northern Ireland Economic Council, research monograph 3, Belfast, 1996

[4] See 'The Civic Forum: a proposal to the first and deputy first ministers designate', New Agenda, Belfast, 1998.

[5] See the chapter by Barnett and Hutchinson in this volume.

[6] 'Northern Ireland: towards a prosperous future', Treasury press release, May 12th 1998

[7] 'Government unveils major increases planned for health and education spending in Northern Ireland', NIO press release, November 4th 1998

[8] See also the moral argument advanced by Paul Teague and Robin Wilson in 'Towards an inclusive society', in *Social Exclusion, Social Inclusion*, DD report 2, Belfast, 1995.

# Autonomy is strength

**John Loughlin**

Autonomy simply means 'self-rule'. In pre-modern times—before the emergence of the nation-state as the dominant form of political organisation—it referred to the seigneuries, bishoprics, monasteries and towns granted the right to self-rule by monarchs and emperors or by virtue of their position in the church.

In its modern sense, it has two primary meanings. As developed by political philosophers from Locke to J S Mill, it refers to the right of *individuals* to dispose of their lives, according to a set of rights, and to choose their form of government and those they wish to represent them. But it may also be understood as the right of *communities*—defined by territory, language, culture or religion—to govern themselves, so that their distinctive features are protected and promoted. This right is especially relevant when these communities are minorities whose cultural, economic, social or geographical characteristics differ from the majorities in which they find themselves.

Normally such communities are also defined by a territorial homeland and they seek primarily political autonomy—"an arrangement aimed at granting to a group that differs from the majority of the population in the state, but that constitutes the majority in a specific region, a means by which it can express its distinct identity". But where distinct minorities do not live in a fixed territory—because they are nomads, such as the *Sami* (Lapp) peoples of northern Europe, or members of a diaspora who have left or lost their homeland, such as Jews, Armenians or *Maghrebins*—they may be recognised as carrying rights (for example, to education according to linguistic or religious custom) exercised on a personal, rather than territorial, basis.[1]

Since it derives from membership of a community, personal is quite different from *individual* autonomy—where certain individual rights take precedence *over* those attaching to the community. It has proved extremely difficult to realise in practice.

Both individual and communitarian/personal autonomy should be understood in relation to the nation-state—that modern form of political organisation, *par excellence*, which originated in the French revolution and developed throughout the 19th century. On the one hand, individual autonomy is at the heart of our understanding of liberal democracy and citizenship. Communitarian autonomy, on the other, often sits uneasily with this individualist understanding and is closely related to political ideologies such as regionalism.

Regionalism developed as a political movement in some European countries towards the end of the 19th century, as a challenge to the liberal-democratic nation-state. The original regionalists were suspicious of human rights and did not like the manifestations of the modern state, such as political parties, elections and parliamentary assemblies. They felt these disrupted the 'natural' communities of the regions, often organised along traditional hierarchical and corporatist lines.

Although contemporary regionalist thought has moved beyond this formulation, there may be tension between rights claimed for the community—in terms of language, education, religious customs and so on—and appeals to individual rights or claims by members of a different community. Regional autonomy may thus create new minorities within. Indeed, the major challenge for institution-builders today is to design institutions that can accommodate all these different concepts of autonomy, and different communities living on the same territory. In some parts of the world—such as the former USSR, India and Africa—the minority situation is incredibly complex and sometimes seems to defy solution.

In western Europe, there tends to be no more than three groups sharing a given sub-state territory: a minority community, a minority within that minority, and another minority more attached to the individual mode of autonomy who experience communitarianism as oppression. In the west, nevertheless, it is common to try to combine the two forms of autonomy, in a system which accepts the declarations on human rights originally formulated as the rights of individuals but also recognises the rights of communities.[2]

Communitarian and individual autonomy do not sit together very easily, however, especially where the community is characterised by strong moral conservatism on issues such as sexual behaviour and orientation. Such considerations are clearly important for societies like Northern Ireland and Scotland. The question has already arisen whether the Scottish Parliament should have responsibility for policy on abortion, while appeals have been made to extend current abortion law in Britain to Northern Ireland.

So 'autonomy' is a complex term, with different meanings not all compatible. And while autonomist movements usually demand modification of the political and administrative structures of nation-states, sometimes they contain nationalist currents which seek to use them to gain full independence. (The Scottish National Party seems to have adopted such a strategy, while in Wales Plaid Cymru has toned down its separatist ambitions.)

But the concept is more complex still. Autonomy must be understood relative to the kind of state in which it operates or in which autonomist demands are made. States may be federal, unitary or 'union'. There are also several kinds of unitary states: centralised unitary, decentralised unitary or regionalised unitary. Furthermore, while all states in western Europe have undergone radical transformations, these are conditioned by particular traditions and political and administrative cultures.[3]

Autonomy is also about diverse relationships to other political institutions. Thus it varies according to: the constitutional position of the autonomous institution and its political competencies; its capacity to control other institutions and to act autonomously outside the nation-state of which it is a part; and its financial and other resources (personnel, expertise, institutional capacity and so on).

Since the concept and practice of autonomy is closely related to the nation-state system, change in the latter will determine the significance of autonomy and the form it will take. Since the second world war, there have been successive paradigm shifts in the relationships between economy, state, society and culture—linked to the changing nature of the European Union.

Nation-states are not disappearing, but their nature, roles and functions are changing. They have divested themselves of many tasks, accumulated particularly in the aftermath of the war. Some have been taken over by the EU, while others have been decentralised to lower levels of government. Furthermore, the neoliberal reform movement of the 80s has modified the institutions, administrative structures and cultures of the state, albeit variably across countries.

The state is, in some senses, stronger than before, but opportunities for new expressions of autonomy and new sets of relationships are emerging in this world of 'multi-level governance'.[4] 'Governance' differs from *government* in being a system of governmental 'steering' involving a range of actors and networks wider than those who are, strictly speaking, members of government institutions. And it is 'multi-level' because several tiers of governance are involved in the new European system: member states, European institutions and, increasingly, sub-national levels and networks of actors.

This represents at the same time new constraints on policy decisions (and therefore on autonomy) *and* new opportunities for policy action on a wider scale and for alliances with a wider range of actors—including, for sub-national governments, not only national governments but also other sub-national governments in other states. It also provides opportunities for institution-building and policy design.

The paradigmatic shifts since the war have expressed, and in turn affected, the value systems of western societies. Although it is difficult to draw hard and fast lines, two major models may be distinguished, as well as a third apparently developing under our eyes (see Table 1): the 'expansive welfare state', from 1945 roughly to the mid-70s; the 'contracting neo-liberal state', from the late 70s to the mid-80s; and the 'enabling communitarian state', arguably from the mid-80s to today.

After the war, almost all western states enjoyed an economic boom, characterised by 'Fordist' (assembly-line) methods of production and reliance on heavy industries like coal and steel. Geographic factors—proximity to coal mines, railways, ports and so on—and infrastructures such as road and rail networks were important. It was thought that the state had to intervene through the nationalisation of key industries—capturing the 'commanding heights of the economy'. Full employment, or something very close, was the goal of economic policy, heavily influenced by Keynesian macro-economic theory.

For decades, it worked, with post-war economic growth boosted by reconstruction and US Marshall aid. Real incomes and living standards rose for most of the population of western European countries. Related to these developments were the first steps toward European integration among the Six.

The origins of the welfare-state model may be traced further back to Bismarck

## Table 1: changing paradigms of state-society relationships, 1945-1997

| | ECONOMY | STATE FEATURES | SOCIETY | CULTURE/VALUES |
|---|---|---|---|---|
| **EXPANSIVE WELFARE STATE** | Fordist production methods; heavy industries: coal and steel; geographical factors of production important; Keynesian approaches to macro-economic management; nationalisation; full employment goal; rise in incomes and living standards; top-down regional policy; founding of EEC. | equality of opportunity; government intervention; progressive income tax; citizens' right to services and expanding definition of 'needs'; centralisation and bureaucratisation of public administration; managerialism in public sector; fiscal overload (1970s); crisis of ungovernability. | freedom of the individual; urbanisation; 'sexual revolution'; expansive definition of human rights; growing importance of mass media; mass travel and tourism; secularisation; student revolutions and 'youth culture'; social engagement. | new values based on freedom and choice; new lifestyles (clothing, living patterns); cosmopolitan culture; regional cultures devalued—reduced to 'folklore' for tourists; regionalist reactions to revalidate their cultures; regional culture seen (by élites) as obstacle to regional development. |
| **CONCTRACTING NEO-LIBERAL STATE** | post-Fordist; deregulation and privatisation; new technologies and systems of communication; new (non-geographical) factors of production; predominance of service industries; globalisation and 'glocalisation'; bottom-up models of regional development; importance of knowledge: the 'learning' and innovative region; accelerated European integration (1985-) | 'hollow', 'elusive', 'anorexic' state; no government intervention; reduction of taxation; privatisation, deregulation; cutting back of services; decentralisation, regionalisation; 'new public management'; 'marketisation' of public services citizens as consumers. | 'no such thing as society' (Thatcher); individualism; glorification of greed; decline of notions of common good and community; fragmentation of communities; creation of an 'underclass' in cities; increasing gap between poor and rich (individual and geographical); | neo-liberal project as propagation of values; rich less willing to pay for welfare services through taxation; reactions to this—eg election of Blair, Jospin, Schroeder; 'remoralisation' in Britain; culture as variable in economic development; new appreciation of and opportunities for regional cultures; Europe of the Cultures 2002 (Flanders). |
| **COMMUNITARIAN/SOCIAL STATE—a new model or neo-liberalism in new clothes?** | acceptance of capitalism and the market; low taxation; end of class struggle; innovative entrepreneurship; social dimension and institutional economics; role for trade unions and local authorities; economic regionalism. | claims to pursue equality of opportunity and social justice but through competition; concept of *enabling* state; no return to old welfare state; slimming down of bureaucracy; new public-private partnership; decentralisation and devolution; revalidation of local authorities and rebuilding local democracy and sense of citizenship; pro-European. | perhaps limits to individualisation and fragmentation; remoralisation of society; concept of community—communitarianism; new approach to law and order issues—'zero tolerance'. | acceptance of individualistic trends; toleration of different life-styles; new concepts of human rights; revalidation of regional and local cultures; personalism. |

in 19th-century Germany and British 'new Liberalism' in the early part of the 20th. Elements can also be found in Catholic social teaching and early Christian democracy. Sweden developed a welfare state in the 30s—the famous Swedish Model. In Britain, it achieved its most complete expression after the war, based on the principles outlined in the Beveridge report of 1942.

Almost all western states adopted welfare systems after the war, though they differed in how they organised and funded them. The British drew upon general taxation while other European countries pursued the social-insurance principle. The Dutch adopted a mixed system.

The success of the welfare state was closely related to the Keynesian-style economic boom. A minority on the left opposed it, criticising its oppressive bureaucracy or its perceived anaesthetising effect on the working class. It was also opposed by a small group of, mostly American, right-wing libertarians, although they had little influence before the 70s.

The welfare state was characterised by:
• a positive and almost optimistic view of the state—governments ought to intervene in the economy and to provide a wide variety of services, in the belief they really could effect social and economic change;
• funding of these services by progressive income tax, as in the UK, or compulsory insurance schemes, as in some other European countries;
• the notion that citizens had a right to these services, within an expanding definition of needs and rights;
• equality of opportunity achieved through centralisation of state services;
• redistribution through centralisation—overall policy would be decided at the centre but regional and local governments had a role and some discretion in administration of these services; and
• application of the principles of equality and state aid at the territorial level, through regional policy manipulating economic levers to 'bring jobs to the workers'.

There were enormous changes in society during this period—the most striking being the exaltation of the individual. This appears paradoxical, given the increasing role and bureaucratisation of the state. There is no real contradiction here, however: the 'emancipation' of the individual was made possible by the security provided by the welfare state.

Key changes were:
• rapid urbanisation;
• changes in family structure;
• secularisation and decline in church-

going, related to individual choice in moral and spiritual issues;
• the sexual revolution associated with 'the pill';
• greater individual freedom and the re-defining of morality in a more liberal direction, with regard to sexual mores, homosexuality and abortion;
• other, pathological, behaviours such as widespread drug-taking and increased alcohol consumption;
• the advent of mass media, especially television with its power to change attitudes and values;
• mass travel and tourism, exposing people to other societies and so relativising aspects of their own previously deemed absolute and unchangeable;
• the student revolutions of the 60s; and
• a great generosity on the part of many young people involved in the 'causes' of the 60s and 70s (the Campaign for Nuclear Disarmament, civil rights, opposition to the Vietnam war and so on).

These social changes were accompanied by changes in values and culture:
• new values based on freedom and choice;
• new lifestyles (clothing and living patterns);
• paradoxically, homogenisation of an increasingly global cosmopolitan culture;
• devaluation of regional cultures, their distinctive languages and values— deemed not to be 'modern', regarded as an obstacle to regional development and reduced to 'folklore' for tourist consumption; and
• contrarily, regionalist reactions to protect and validate these cultures from extinction by homogenising forces.

In the late 60s and early 70s, the Keynes/Beveridge model of state, economy and society in Britain, and its Christian- and social-democratic counterparts on continental Europe, entered into crisis.

The post-war boom ended as oil prices spiralled out of control and 'stagflation' (stagnation-plus-inflation) became endemic. Trade unions were routinely blamed for poor productivity and 'excessive' wage demands, and unemployment soared. 'Fiscal overload' emerged as rising social costs became increasingly difficult to meet out of general taxation, which itself became deeply unpopular. Some authors, mostly on the right, claimed there was a crisis of 'ungovernability': government itself had become too big.

Despite these problems—or, perhaps, because of them—capitalism was successfully reinvented, as a new, 'post-Fordist' era dawned, supported by new information and communication technologies. Service industries—insurance, banking, education, tourism and so on—predominated over the older, 'smokestack' heavyweights. Mass, assembly-line production tended to be replaced by batch production for segmented markets, or 'flexible specialisation'.

This often meant nothing more than low-paid and insecure employment for vulnerable groups like working-class women and migrants. In countries such as the Netherlands, however, there has developed a genuine approach to flexible working practices by all sectors of the workforce, from senior managers to those in more humble positions. This seems to have led to real increases in productivity, closely connected to a more committed and contented workforce.

This shift away from heavy industry, plus new communications systems and technologies, has at one level rendered geography no longer so important (although centres of decision-making—political, economic or financial—still tend to cluster around traditional capitals and, in Europe, the 'golden triangle' core of the EU). Nevertheless, globalisation, while liberating economic activity from dependence on spatial factors, has reaffirmed the importance of territory in a new sense.

First, in a rather banal way, footloose capital roving the globe will sometimes take into account the attractiveness of a particular location. Now infrastructure includes not only transport networks but also the quality of communications and the skills of the workforce; the quality of the environment will also figure. Secondly, globalisation is increasingly related, through the ugly neologism 'glocalisation', to the emergence of regional and local foci of production, which may not coincide with those of the Fordist period.

This change has led to a new understanding of regional economic development, which is today based on 'bottom-up' and more 'endogenous' approaches geared to achieving the status of an 'intelligent' or 'learning' region.[5] These emphasise non-hierarchical organisation and the importance of innovation and flexibility in production. Progress is achieved through networks—partnership, team-work and subsidiarity—rather than top-down directives. It is claimed that this model underlies the success of regions such as Emilia-Romagna and Baden-Württemberg—though it may also be that this approach masks the withdrawal of the central state from providing aid to regions in need.

It is no accident that, in the neoliberal period, the then European Community became an important economic factor. First, its 'relaunch' in the 80s, via the European Council and the European Commission headed by Jacques Delors, was a direct response to the economic crisis of the 70s. The deep recession, massive unemployment, flagging productivity, lack of technological inventiveness, inflation and social unrest of this period were perceived by industrial and political élites as putting Europe at a disadvantage in the new global markets, increasingly dominated by Japan and the US. These élites recognised that individual countries—even large ones like Germany—could not meet the challenge alone; they had to do so together.

It was Mr Delors, as incoming president of the European Commission in 1985, who saw that the completion of the single market by 1992 could be the means of galvanising the different member states together, and thus renewing European integration after many years of 'sclerosis'. The single market led to the Maastricht treaty, economic and monetary union and the prospect of a single currency, the euro. Also signalled was a European Central Bank, taking over the monetary policy of those members participating in the euro (but not other economic instruments, which remain the responsibility of national governments). What all this means is a strengthening of the trend towards much greater autonomy of the financial and economic sectors, with much less intervention by political institutions.

As a response to the economic crisis of the 70s, the neo-liberal approach to the state was developed by such economists and philosophers as Milton Friedman and Friedrich von Hayek, James Buchanan and Michael Nozick. They promoted the 'minimalist' or 'nightwatchman' state, intervening in society and the economy only when absolutely necessary—though, strictly speaking, these authors were anarchists since they wished to see states disappear completely. They also believed that the market, understood as the arena of free exchange between individuals, could provide the range of services hitherto provided by the state more efficiently and effectively—a direct contradiction of the welfare-state idea.

Once dismissed as crackpot, Ronald Reagan and Margaret Thatcher deployed the model in a way that touched popular chords, leading to the UK becoming, for almost two decades, a laboratory of governmental reform and social engineering on an immense scale. Most other European countries followed suit, though not always to the same extent or in the same way.[6] The neo-liberal approach also enjoyed a period of great popularity in the former Soviet-bloc countries after the collapse of the USSR, as well as in Latin American countries which made a transition to democracy in the 80s.

The principles underlying the neo-liberal model of the state amounted to a reversal of those underpinning the welfare state:
- the key unit was not society, whose common good was pursued, but the individual (as in Mrs Thatcher's notorious disclaimer that there was any such thing as society);
- the notion of the 'citizen', participating equally in government with other citizens through representative democracy regardless of economic and social standing, was replaced by the 'consumer', who got what they could pay for (hence, again, Mrs Thatcher's ideal of a 'car-owning democracy');
- inequality, whether between individuals or territories, was accepted—even promoted—as opposed to egalitarian social and regional policies;
- government intervention was deemed a 'bad thing', since always inefficient and wasteful, whereas the private sector was assumed to provide better and cheaper services;
- it was held that, where possible, services such as pensions should be funded via private (non-compulsory) insurance schemes, so that general taxation could be progressively reduced;
- 'new public management' approaches—usually borrowed from the private sector—were implemented, radically reforming the structure and procedures of the civil service (public spending continued to rise despite these reforms, however, while quality of services, especially education and health, seriously declined);
- there was ambivalence on Europe—on the one hand, an acceptance of the single market (after all, Mrs Thatcher signed the Single European Act, which seemed to be about liberating market forces), yet, on the other, a distrust of the 'federalist' tendencies of integration and the more social dimensions of Europe; and
- with the exception of the UK, government was further regionalised and decentralised (paradoxically, Mrs Thatcher's attack on the state and bureaucracy led to one of the most centralised periods in British history, with the creation of a multitude of bureaucracies presiding over health and educational services and unaccountable quangos).

Once again, there were several significant social shifts:
- the individual became absolute—understood as the bearer of a bundle of rights but with few obligations or duties;
- morality was individualised as lifestyle choice—as against perceived interference by government, church or any other association;
- financial success was glorified, whatever the consequences for others, in

contrast to the previous discretion about private wealth;
- a sense of society and community declined, with associated recruitment difficulties for traditional associations such as parties or churches;
- established communities fragmented or even experienced moral collapse; and
- in the UK in particular, class and geographical divisions widened: rich *versus* poor, the south-east *versus* the rest, the Celtic fringe *versus* England.

The neo-liberal project meant the propagation of new values, or what were sometimes claimed as reawakened older ones (the ambiguity around individualism and 'Victorian values' in Britain allowed, to some extent, of a 'remoralisation' of public debate, after some particularly gruesome serial killings and child murders):
- the rich were less willing to pay for welfare services through general taxation and, in the US and some European countries, this led to tax revolts—though the elections of Tony Blair in Britain, Lionel Jospin in France and Gerard Schröder in Germany might be interpreted as signs that many in these countries feel the neoliberal project has gone too far in devalorising the social dimension;
- there was a growing appreciation of 'culture' as a variable in economic development—probably connected to the realisation of the importance of knowledge and learning in the new paradigm;
- there was a new, related appreciation of the opportunities for regional cultures—the Catalans promoted this with great success; and
- a new way of conceiving Europe as a mosaic of cultures was developed, particularly by the Flemish government with its concept of cultural diversity.

After nearly two decades of Thatcherite restructuring of the UK, the British people decided, on May 1st 1997, that they had had enough.

Thus began an era of reform with a government, led by Mr Blair, whose ideas and ideology mark a significant departure not only from Thatcherism but also from the welfare state, towards an enabling, communitarian model. During the election, many critics of new Labour—from both right and left—claimed there was little to choose between what Mr Blair proposed and what the Tories had already provided. Although there are continuities in some of the policies of new Labour, there are also significant differences—the most important being the recovery of a sense of community, lost under Mrs Thatcher and her successor, John Major.

In this regard, Mr Blair has had intellectual gurus on which to draw, notably the communitarianism developed by Amitai Etzioni, Charles Taylor and John McMurray, as well as Christian socialism. It remains to be seen whether the Blairite model will be propagated throughout Europe, in the manner of Thatcherism and as Mr Blair himself would like, under the banner of a 'third way' between old-style welfarism and neo-liberalism.

Certainly, there has been a great deal of interest in the Blair style, notably reflected in Mr Schröder's election campaign for the chancellorship. But 'Blairism' probably owes more to thinkers and experiments in the US associated with Bill Clinton and the 'reinvention of government' movement.

It is in the approach to economic issues that new Labour most resembles old Tories. There are, however, some differences of nuance. New Labour accepts the notion of 'institutionalist economics', as opposed to the neo-liberal idea of a pure market situation. But it is also true that new Labour accepts capitalism in theory as well as in practice, no longer seeking to capture the 'commanding heights' to institute a classless society.

Unlike the Tories, though, Labour accepts there is a social dimension to the economy—in terms not only of social protection but also of bringing the socially excluded into the labour market. Also accepted is a new role for trade unions and local authorities in economic development, now seen as partners rather than enemies—though they will remain under the direction of government, not *vice versa*. Economic regionalism also seems to be a key component of Labour's strategy.

The government agrees with the Tories that there should be no increase in personal taxation. But to some extent, while relying on thinkers from the US, new Labour thinking on the economy comes close to the social-market model of Germany and the Netherlands, particularly the latter.

As regards the state, again there are continuities and changes. New Labour claims it is pursuing equality of opportunity and social justice, but asserts these will be best served through competition and the pursuit of excellence rather than levelling down. With regard to state-economy relations, however, there is talk of a new public-private partnership: the private sector is not necessarily better (one of the dogmas of neo-liberalism) and the public sector can provide useful models for policy in certain areas.

At the centre of the government's reforms is a programme of radical devolution for Scotland, Wales and Northern Ireland, as well as London and (where desired) the English regions. It wishes to see relations between the centre, region and locality based on collaboration rather than conflict—as with the unions and the churches. The House of Lords will also be reformed, and this may be tied to the wider territorial reforms by allowing a measure of territorial representation in an elected upper chamber.

By these reforms Labour wishes to restore a sense of citizenship rather than consumerism, but its ideal might be seen as communitarian democracy—the decentralisation proposals are a reflection of this goal. New Labour is pro-European, and many of its themes fit easily into the European traditions of social and Christian democracy, federalism and regionalism, but it still opposes a fully-fledged European federation and still defends what it perceives to be Britain's interests.

In many respects, society itself has not changed significantly since the crisis of the neo-liberal model: individualism and fragmentation remain evident. But the wave of centre-left election victories does seem to indicate a new mood: the days of Essex man and woman, selfishly pursuing their own interests, appear to have peaked. The public in Britain, France and Germany seem to be yearning for a more moral approach and the restoration of some kind of community life.

The success of Mr Blair and new Labour has been at least in part a result of having read correctly, and capitalised upon, this new mood—just as Mrs Thatcher did in the early years of her régime. According to opinion polls, there is a greater willingness on the part of ordinary citizens to pay for social welfare measures through slightly higher taxation, and a great concern about issues such as the environment, famine and injustice.

What is really new in this period is the explosion of new technologies connected with the internet and other forms of communications. The costs of communication are tumbling and the younger generations are becoming more and more adept in using the new technologies.

As to culture and values, there is a continuing acceptance of individualist trends and of a variety of life-styles (for example, gays seem to have found a new acceptance), but this is tempered by the new emphasis on 'community'. At least, there is a sense that certain valuable forms of community have been lost and that there is a worrying disintegration of society. There is also a concern that decisions are taken at too great a distance from the ordinary citizen.

Nevertheless, these concerns do not seem to be translating into political or social action at local level. And the idea that the internet may prove a means of improving local democracy is something of a pipe-dream; rather, for the moment it seems a powerful means of reinforcing individualism and fragmentation.

Three paradigms of economy/state/society/culture relationships have for analytical purposes been identified, associated with distinct approaches to public policy and administration and distinct value systems. This is not to suggest clear cut-off points: the different paradigms fade into each other, with some features of later models anticipated earlier and aspects of prior paradigms retained in subsequent periods.

It is also extremely difficult to isolate cause and effect. Much of the dynamic behind these shifts seems to have originated in economic developments and in the avalanche of new technologies over the last 40 years, now accelerating at an incredible rate. These economic changes are, however, conditioned by values and social attitudes and by forms of state activity and design. What we appear to have witnessed is the emergence of a new kind of state, with new roles and functions and new relationships with other levels of government, and with the private sector and society.

The macro-context of globalisation and Europeanisation is important. In fact, Europeanisation is both a response to the threat of globalisation and an expression of it. There is thus a need to rethink political concepts and practices—nation and state (and their combination into nation-state), democracy and representative government—and institutions. We are approaching the 21st century with political and administrative institutions inherited from the 19th-century nation-state, built on the principles of the 18th-century enlightenment.

All 15 members of the EU are liberal democracies which share a common history of value formation and institutional development. At the core of the concept of liberal democracy is the notion that sovereignty derives from 'the people' rather than God or monarchs. The people and 'the nation' have become synonymous since the French revolution established the principle that the people, or nation, freely choose their representatives, who meet in assemblies to decide on the nation's affairs. Political executives and administrative bureaucracies are accountable to these assemblies, and are meant to execute faithfully the assembly's decisions.

This system of democratic practice also operates at the sub-national level—regional, provincial, local or sub-local—with all states (even Luxembourg!) having elected governments at some or all of these levels. The actual exercise of power is not, however, always consonant with its constitutional definition: all western political systems are characterised by great complexity, inscribed in a multitude of relationships and networks. Nevertheless, politics still occurs within the basic parameters of liberal democracy as outlined.

Despite sharing these common principles, however, modern democracies are also characterised by great variety in their institutional expression. First, the meaning and history of the concept of democracy vary across countries, as does the concept of the state itself.[7] These variations have given rise to different ways of conceiving the relationship between state and civil society and, in particular, centre-region relations.[8]

The French tradition, for example, tends towards a concept of the state based on the abstract 'citizen' represented in the National Assembly, without the mediation of intermediary bodies such as churches, trade unions or other corporations. It was in France that the Jacobin notion of the one and indivisible republic triumphed in the form of the centralised, unitary state. It was here, too, that the coupling of nation and state into the nation-state was first developed and became the most advanced example of political and administrative organisation in the 19th century, much admired by nationalists in newly emerging nations such as Greece, Ireland, Spain and Portugal.

The Germanic tradition, on the other hand, posits a close interpenetration of state and society and encourages intermediary bodies to play a role in state activities. This might be traced to Hegelian concepts of the state-society relationship and has been associated with an indigenous federalist tradition in Germany going back to the last century (even if post-war federalism was imposed by the victorious allies). The centralised Weimar republic and the period of the Third Reich might be regarded as aberrations from this tradition. In the Scandinavian tradition, local government has an important role, leading to the development of the *de*centralised, unitary state.

Britain combines aspects of the pre-modern state (an overarching monarchy ruling over several nations—England, Scotland and Wales and, until 1920, Ireland) and a modern, centralised, bureaucratic state. The key component of the British model is the supremacy of Parliament, which claims absolute sovereignty over the constituent parts of the kingdom. Thus, it is a misnomer to describe the UK as a 'nation-state', even as a unitary state. Rather, it is more accurate to describe it as a 'union' or 'multi-national' state. In this system—

## Table 2: centre-region relations in EU member states

| Type of state | States | Political regions[1] | Admin/planning regions[2] | Right to participate in national policy | Right to conclude foreign treaties[3] | Control over sub-regional authorities |
|---|---|---|---|---|---|---|
| Federal | Austria | Länder (10) | | Yes | Yes (but limited) | Yes (not absolute) |
| | Belgium | Communities[4] (3) | | Yes | Yes (but limited) | No |
| | | Regions (3) | | Yes | Yes (but limited) | Yes (not absolute) |
| | Germany | Länder (16) | | Yes | Yes (but limited) | Yes (not absolute) |
| Regionalised unitary | Italy[5] | Regioni[7] (20) | | Consultative | No | Yes |
| | France | Régions[8] (21) | | Consultative | No | No |
| | Spain | Comunidades Autonomas (17) | | No | No | Yes |
| | United Kingdom[6] | Scottish Parliament Welsh National Assembly Northern Ireland Assembly | English standard regions | No with regard to English regions Still unclear with regard to Scotland, Wales and NI | No at present, but may evolve | Yes in Scotland and NI No in Wales (so far) |
| Decentralised unitary | Denmark | Faroese Islands | Groups of Amter | No | No | No |
| | Finland | Aaland Islands | Counties have regional planning function | No | No (but has seat in Nordic Council) | Yes |
| | Netherlands | | Landsdelen | Consultative | No | No |
| | Sweden | | Regional administrative bodies | No | No | No |
| Centralised unitary | Greece | | Development regions (13) | No | No | No |
| | Republic of Ireland | | Regional authorities (8) | No | No | No |
| | Luxembourg | NA | | NA | NA | NA |
| | Portugal | Island regions[9] | | No | No | No |

[1] This refers to regions and nations (as in Scotland, Wales, Catalonia, the Basque Country and Galicia) with a directly elected assembly to which a regional executive is accountable.
[2] This refers to regions without a directly elected assembly which exist primarily for administrative/planning purposes.
[3] There is a sharp distinction between the federal and non-federal states in this regard; however, the majority of non-federal states may allow regions to engage in international activities with the approval and under the control of the national government.
[4] The Flemish linguistic Community and the Flanders economic Region have decided to form one body; the Walloon Community and Region remain separate.
[5] Italy is undergoing a process of political reform which involves the transformation of the old state into a new kind of state with some federal features. Although the position of the regions will be strengthened, it will not become a federal state such as Germany or Belgium.
[6] The United Kingdom was, until the referenda in Scotland and Wales in September 1997, a highly centralised 'union' state. But the positive outcome of the referenda means there will be a Scottish Parliament and a Welsh National Assembly by 1999. A referendum in 1998 on a Greater London Authority with an elected mayor was also successful and this is seen as a precursor to possible regional assemblies in England. The successful outcome of the Northern Ireland 'peace process' means there will be a Northern Ireland Assembly as well as other new institutions linking the different nations and peoples of the islands.
[7] In Italy there are 17 'ordinary' regions and 5 with a special statute because of their linguistic or geographical peculiarities: Sicily, Sardinia, Trentino-Alto Adige (South Tyrol to its large German-speaking population), Val d'Aosta and Friuli-Venezia Giulia.
[8] There are 21 regions on mainland France; to these one must add Corsica and the overseas departments and territories (the 'DOM-TOM'). Since 1991, Corsica has had a special statute and is officially a 'collectivité territoriale' rather than a region. The TOM, too, have special statutes and one of them, New Caledonia, has recently (May 1998) been permitted to accede to independence within 20 years.
[9] Portugal, while making provision in its constitution for regionalisation, has so far only granted autonomy to the island groups of the Azores and Madeira. The mainland remains highly centralised. A government-sponsored proposal that eight planning regions be established was defeated in a referendum in November 1998.

unlike the French, for example—there was (until the new Labour devolution programme) a high degree of political centralisation, combined with much administrative idiosyncrasy.

Nevertheless, there is not an infinite variety of states in western Europe and it is possible to place most of them in a limited number of categories (Table 2). A basic distinction should be made between federal and unitary (or, in the case of the UK, union) states.

Federations themselves differ. Some, such as the US and Switzerland, were created as the result of centripetal tendencies: distinct, already existing political units came together for mutual benefit. Others, such as Belgium, are the product of centrifugal forces—the failure of communities within a unitary state to live together satisfactorily. Such centrifugal tendencies can of course lead to the break-up of unitary states (like the secession of 26 counties of Ireland in 1920-21) as well as federal ones (such as Czechoslovakia's 'velvet divorce').

Unitary states, too, may be sub-divided, as indicated earlier.

When applied to sub-national government, autonomy has a number of dimensions. These are: the legal position—whether this is defined constitutionally or through ordinary legislation; the political competencies accorded to the sub-national level; the degree of participation in national policy-making; the possibility of engaging in activities beyond the frontiers of the national territory; the degree of control over other sub-national levels; and, finally, the degree of financial autonomy from, or dependence on, the national government.

The constitutional position of sub-national government might be represented as a spectrum, with constitutionally entrenched guarantees at one end and simple legislative guarantees at the other. All federal states are examples of the former, with formal recognition of the level immediately below the federal (the *Länder* in Germany, the states in the US, the provinces in Canada and so on). There is not always a constitutional guarantee, however, of levels of government below this (for example, the *Kreise* in Germany or the counties and cities in the US). Spain and Italy, regionalised unitary states, do constitutionally guarantee the existence of the autonomous communities and *regioni* respectively. The French constitution, meanwhile, recognises the departments and communes but not the regions, which exist only through legislation.

Generally speaking, constitutional rather than simple statutory recognition gives the sub-national body extra strength and legitimacy—in other words, increases its autonomy.

In the UK, with its tradition of 'parliamentary sovereignty' and lack of a written constitution, sub-national government has been extremely weak, as the 'proroguing' (in effect, abolition) of the old Stormont Parliament in 1972 and the abolition of the Greater London Council in 1986 illustrate—both disappeared overnight by a simple act of the Westminster Parliament. This problem is not solved in the current devolution programme, as Westminster still retains ultimate sovereignty and may override the decisions of any of the new bodies.[9] Clearly, there is scope for bringing the UK's constitution into line with the new political realities.

Political competencies are defined by the constitution or by enabling legislation. There are two basic approaches: the central state defines those powers it reserves for itself or it provides a detailed list of competencies that fall within the sub-national remit. Generally speaking, federal states follow the former course while unitary states adopt the latter. At the local government level, however, many unitary states—for example, in the Scandinavian tradition—grant a general competence. In the UK, by contrast, local government has traditionally been based on the principle of *ultra vires*: local authorities are unable to go beyond the powers detailed in parliamentary legislation.

The recent devolution reforms have modified this approach with regard to the new assemblies. In these cases, it is the residual powers to be exercised by the Westminster Parliament that are listed (the traditional powers of a federal government: foreign affairs, defence, finance and macro-economic policy). Nevertheless, with regard to sub-national government in all parts of the UK, the *ultra vires* rule still applies, requiring complex schedules to be inserted in the Scotland, Wales and Northern Ireland bills to determine a 'devolution issue', ultimately referable to the Judicial Committee of the Privy Council for decision.

Federal systems usually have institutional mechanisms allowing the sub-federal units to exercise an influence on national policy-making. The most advanced example is the German *Bundesrat*, the upper chamber in which the *Länder* are represented and which has an important influence on the legislative activities of the *Bundestag* or federal parliament. In the US, the Senate plays a similar role and allows the states to be equally represented (two senators from each, regardless of population).

Some unitary states have similar mechanisms. In France, for example, the Senate explicitly gives representation to local authorities. In Italy, the regions are represented by the *Conferenza Permanente Stato-regioni*.

Involvement in national policy-making may, however, have different meanings. On the one hand, it may be purely consultative—in Italy, for example, national legislators are not obliged to modify their proposals as a result. On the other hand, as with the German *Bundesrat*, it may indeed mean the capacity to change proposed legislation. In many states, there is no formal mechanism for involvement in national policy-making but informal mechanisms may exist. In unitary states such as the Republic of Ireland and Greece, and in parts of Italy and France, local interests are mediated to the centre via a clientelisic system of notables, whether individuals or parties.

In the UK, the interests of the Celtic periphery are represented to some extent by the secretaries of state holding seats in the cabinet. There is also a territorial dimension to the party system, with Labour and the Liberal Democrats to some extent representing the periphery in Scotland and Wales, as well as parts of England (even if this broke down during the long period of Tory rule).

The devolution programme partly addresses this problem by granting assemblies/parliaments to the Celtic regions/nations—and, perhaps eventually, to the English regions. It is still unclear, however, how these bodies will be represented at the UK level and what influence they will have over policy-making. The proposed reform of the Lords does offer an opportunity to institutionalise regional representation but there are no proposals to do so.

The general lesson to be drawn is that the greater the involvement in national policy-making, the greater the degree of autonomy.

International activities represent the area that touches most closely upon the traditional concept of 'national sovereignty'. International relations are deemed the exclusive prerogative of nation-state governments. The 'realist' school of international relations conceived states as discrete units, interacting like a set of billiard balls: there might be different ways in which the balls were configured but there could be little interpenetration between them.

Current thinking has largely dispensed with this approach, recognising that the line between the domestic and the international has become blurred. This is most striking in the EU where national sovereignty has been considerably modified, constitutionally and in practice. This is true even if there is still no single common foreign and security policy superseding the foreign policies of the member states.

There is great complexity in this area. First, in some states, mainly the federations, sub-federal units may engage officially in foreign activities—even signing treaties with other governments in fields that fall within the competence of that level of government. Secondly, some regions have established institutional arrangements with their neighbours across borders. In most cases, these associations exist as entities of private rather than public law, since the latter forbids such activity by any level of government other than the central state.

Thirdly, there is the specific Four Motors of Europe association (comprising Baden-Württemberg, Catalonia, Lombardy and Rhône-Alpes), which exists primarily for the exchange of business information and encouragement of investment in the four regions. Fourthly, there are many inter-regional associations which represent the interests of regions generally, as with the Assembly of European Regions, or specific geographical or economic sectors, such as the Conference of Peripheral Maritime Regions or the Association of Cross-Border Regions. Although composed of regional and local authorities, these are private associations and do not have constitutional recognition at the EU or national levels.

The EU's Committee of the Regions is in a different category. Set up in 1994 as a result of the Treaty on European Union, it is an officially constituted EU body (but not institution[10]) which exists to give regions and local authorities an official say in EU policy-making. Although the committee is purely consultative—and something of a disappointment to those who had hoped for a strong 'Europe of regions'—it does represent a breakthrough for sub-national authorities in the EU.

A final category of international activity of sub-national authorities has been termed 'para-diplomacy'. This involves sub-national governments setting up offices in Brussels or in other countries, within and outside the EU. A striking example of this has been the Catalan government under its president Jordi Pujol, very active on the international scene.

The attitude of central authorities to this varies greatly. When the activities are officially sanctioned by the federal states there is, of course, no problem. Often, the central government will try to ensure cross-border links or relations with the EU are kept tightly under its control, with arrangements subject to its approval. At times, there has been tension between sub-national authorities and national governments which perceive the former to be impinging upon their prerogatives in international affairs—this has been especially evident in Spain over Mr Pujol's Catalan activism.

On the other hand, central governments sometimes encourage paradiplomacy, as it may bring great economic benefits to the region, and therefore the country as a whole. This is true even in the Spanish case, where Madrid and Catalonia often collaborate on the European scene.

Clearly, the greater the capacity to act on the international scene—whether officially approved by the central government or not—the greater, again, the degree of autonomy.

In federal systems, there is normally no direct relationship between federal and local government. Normally the sub-federal level exercises legal and financial control over the local—this is certainly the case in Germany, Austria and Belgium. There is a strong drive by the Flemish government to exercise complete control over the provinces and communes—even to 'recapture' the (formerly Flemish) city of Brussels, which though contained within the boundaries of Flanders is officially bilingual.

In some regionalised unitary states, such as Spain and Italy, the autonomous community or *regione* exercises control over the provinces and municipalities. In the Spanish case, however, there are differences among the ACs: in Catalonia, the *Generalitat* (the regional government) has tended to impose its hegemony over all other levels in the region, while in the Basque country there is a degree of decentralisation, with the provinces playing an important role. In France, the regions have no control over the *départements* and municipalities.

In some cases, large cities have the resources and expertise to escape from the control of the constitutionally higher level of government. In Catalonia, there is conflict between Barcelona and the *Generalitat*, exacerbated by the city having been Socialist while the *Generalitat* has been *Convergencia i Unio* (centre-right Catalan nationalist). This issue is important for the new, decentralised UK, where internal relations within the different territories are still rather unclear.

The Scottish Parliament, it seems, will exercise legal and financial control over Scottish local authorities. It appears the Welsh Assembly will have a much looser arrangement: its relationship to the local authorities has not been clarified. It is also unclear what the position will be in Northern Ireland, where district councils have few powers. How they will develop in the future is largely in the hands of the new Assembly.

The Greater London Authority will

not exercise control over the London boroughs but will, instead, have a planning and co-ordination role in defined areas—rather similar to the position of the French regions with regard to the *départements* and municipalities. Finally, although elected regional governments in England will not come into existence in the lifetime of this Parliament—if they ever do—there will be new regional chambers and regional development agencies in the English standard regions. Clearly, these bodies will be unable to exercise any hegemony over the existing local authorities and their members will be composed, at least partially, of elected members from these authorities. But the issue will arise if, and when, English regional governments are set up.

Again, a simple conclusion might be drawn: regional autonomy increases if the sub-national government has control over other levels of government, while it escapes from such controls itself.

Financial resources underlie political and administrative autonomy. Whatever the constitutional or legal provisions, these are of little account if the regional or local authority does not have the resources to give them expression. Once again, it is the federal systems where the position is clearest: generally, sub-national authorities have substantial financial resources, with their own tax-raising powers. In recent years, however, there has been much criticism in Germany of the degree of control over finances exercised by the federal government and the *Länder* have struggled to retain their financial autonomy.

In non-federal states the situation varies. In small countries like the Republic of Ireland, Greece and Portugal, local financial control is very weak as funding is usually in the form of block grants from central government—which often defines the ways these can be spent. In other cases, while much local-authority funding may come in this form, there is some local taxation and there is more discretion on expenditure, with local authorities allowed to establish their own priorities within the band of their competencies. This is largely the case in France, where financial transfers are made on the basis of contracts signed between the state and local authorities. Finally, local finance may come largely from local revenues supplemented by central grants. In this case, the local authorities may decide not only on priorities but also on amounts to be raised.

Autonomy should be understood as a multi-faceted, complex and dynamic concept.

First, it may be understood as either individual or communitarian autonomy.

The individualist concept has underlain the value system of the modern nation-state while the communitarian version has usually been seen as in opposition. Today, however, it is necessary to combine the two understandings—a concern with the rights of the individual with a concern for the rights of communities, especially minority communities. This is extremely difficult to achieve.

The form and significance of the nation-state—in which autonomy is sought or expressed—has been changing in responses to pressures within and without. There has been a progression of three paradigms—the expanding welfare state, the contracting neo-liberal state and the enabling communitarian state—marked by shifting relationships between the economy, state, society and culture. These paradigm shifts affect the nature of political systems and public policies and, in particular, the position of sub-national authorities such as regions.

The state itself is being transformed and this has consequences for the 'nation-state'. These two concepts need to be uncoupled and each has to be redefined more exactly in terms of the changing dynamics of contemporary societies and economies—changes also affecting the notion of autonomy.

The brief survey above of experiences across western Europe shows great variety. Yet what these states have in common is similar processes of change, even if these express themselves differently. This means that the realities of autonomy, along its various dimensions, are also in a state of flux.

New constraints are being imposed on all levels of government by economic globalisation and competition. But for sub-national levels this also represents a new 'window of opportunity' to increase their actual autonomy (whatever their constitutional status). As we move from government to govern*ance*, there is a great need to design new institutions which may more fully express these new realities and relationships.

Such institutions will no longer be simply the top-down, hierarchical bureaucracies of the past; they will be characterised more by horizontal, network-like features, in which policy initiatives emerge from below. Yet the old systems of representative democracy (government) will not disappear, the challenge is to integrate the new systems of governance into these older ones.

In other words, we need also to rethink our concept of democracy—and therefore of autonomy itself. ■

**Footnotes**

[1] Ruth Lapidoth, *Autonomy: Flexible Solutions to Ethnic Conflicts*, United States Institute of

Peace Press, Washington DC, 1997, pp 33, 37

[2] ibid, pp 37-40

[3] J Loughlin and B G Peters, 'State traditions and regional administrative reform', in M Keating and Loughlin eds, *The Political Economy of Regionalism*, Frank Cass, London, 1997

[4] *Continentally Challenged: Securing Northern Ireland's Place in the European Union*, Democratic Dialogue report 5, Belfast, 1997, pp 15-17

[5] P Cooke and K Morgan, *The Associational Economy: Firms, Regions, and Innovation*, Oxford University Press, 1998

[6] V Wright ed, *Privatisation in Western Europe: Pressures, Problems, and Paradoxes*, Pinter, London, 1994

[7] K Dyson, *The State Tradition in Western Europe*, Martin Robertson, Oxford, 1980

[8] Loughlin and Peters, op cit

[9] Thus the Northern Ireland Bill implementing the Belfast agreement makes clear at §18(1) that "The executive power in Northern Ireland shall continue to be vested in Her Majesty" and at §43(1) that "Her Majesty may by Order in Council prorogue or further prorogue the Assembly."

[10] In EU legal terminology, only the Council of Ministers, the European Commission, the European Parliament, the European Court of Justice and the member states are recognised as 'institutions' of the community; the Committee of the Regions, the Court of Audit, and the Economic and Social Committee are 'bodies' with a lesser constitutional status. The Committee of the Regions attempted, unsuccessfully, to have its status upgraded by the 1996 intergovernmental conference which led to the Amsterdam treaty.

# Bang for the buck

**Vani Borooah**[1]

The last three decades saw the emergence, in the major industrialised countries, of the growth of government. Governmental activities came to play a major role in economic affairs.

Table 1 shows government expenditure as a percentage of gross domestic product in seven countries of the Organisation for Economic Co-operation and Development, for selected years during 1960-90. In each case, this proportion was higher in 1990 than in 1970, and considerably greater than in 1960.

Table 2 shows the shares, in GDP, of the main economic categories of government expenditure for five countries (USA, Japan, Germany, France and the UK) for the years 1979 and 1990. Two items dominate:
- cash transfers to the personal sector, mainly as pensions and other social security benefits, and
- government consumption of goods and services, itself dominated by the public-sector wage bill.

The largest item in all cases was spending on income transfers, varying from 32 per cent of government expenditure in the USA and the UK to nearly 40 per cent in Germany. These were, in turn, dominated by transfers for income maintenance, predominantly retirement pensions.

**Table 1: government expenditure as proportion of GDP in seven OECD countries (%)**

|  | 1960 | 1970 | 1980 | 1990 |
|---|---|---|---|---|
| United States | 27.7 | 32.4 | 33.7 | 37.0 |
| Germany | 32.0 | 38.6 | 48.3 | 46.0 |
| France | 35.7 | 38.9 | 46.1 | 50.4 |
| United Kingdom | 32.4 | 39.0 | 44.6 | 42.9 |
| Italy | 32.1 | 34.3 | 41.7 | 53.2 |
| Canada | 28.9 | 35.7 | 40.5 | 46.4 |
| Sweden | 31.1 | 43.7 | 61.6 | 61.5 |
| Unweighted average | 31.4 | 37.5 | 45.2 | 48.2 |
| Standard deviation | 2.6 | 3.7 | 9.1 | 7.8 |

Source: OECD, *National Accounts*

### Table 2: government outlays by economic category (% GDP)

|  | United States 1979 | 1990 | Change | Japan 1979 | 1990 | Change | Germany 1979 | 1990 | Change | France 1979 | 1990 | Change | United Kingdom 1979 | 1990 | Change |
|---|---|---|---|---|---|---|---|---|---|---|---|---|---|---|---|
| Total current disbursements | 30.4 | 35.2 | 4.8 | 23.9 | 24.7 | 0.8 | 42.4 | 42.3 | 0.0 | 41.4 | 46.6 | 5.2 | 39.2 | 38.1 | -1.1 |
| Government consumption | 17.0 | 18.3 | 1.2 | 9.7 | 9.0 | -0.7 | 19.6 | 18.5 | -1.1 | 17.6 | 18.3 | 0.7 | 19.7 | 20.0 | 0.3 |
| Subsidies | 0.4 | 0.2 | -0.2 | 1.3 | 0.7 | -0.6 | 2.2 | 1.9 | -0.3 | 2.0 | 1.6 | -0.3 | 2.4 | 1.1 | -1.3 |
| Social security and other transfers | 10.2 | 11.5 | 1.3 | 10.3 | 11.2 | 1.0 | 18.9 | 19.3 | 0.4 | 20.4 | 23.5 | 3.1 | 12.8 | 13.7 | 0.9 |
| Debt interest payments | 2.8 | 5.2 | 2.4 | 2.6 | 3.8 | 1.1 | 1.7 | 2.6 | 1.0 | 1.4 | 3.1 | 1.7 | 4.4 | 3.4 | -1.0 |
| Government investment | 1.7 | 1.6 | -0.1 | 6.3 | 5.0 | -1.3 | 3.2 | 2.3 | -1.0 | 3.1 | 3.3 | 0.2 | 2.6 | 2.1 | -0.5 |
| Capital transfers | -0.4 | -0.2 | 0.1 | 0.5 | 0.0 | -0.4 | 1.8 | 1.1 | -0.6 | 0.4 | 0.2 | -0.2 | 0.7 | -2.9 | -3.6 |
| Other transfers | -0.1 | 0.4 | 0.5 | 0.9 | 1.0 | 0.1 | 0.2 | 0.1 | -0.1 | 0.1 | 0.1 | 0.0 | 0.0 | 0.0 | 0.0 |
| Total | 31.7 | 37.0 | 5.2 | 31.6 | 30.7 | -0.9 | 47.6 | 45.8 | -1.8 | 45.0 | 50.2 | 5.2 | 42.5 | 42.9 | 0.3 |

Many economic and political commentators came to regard this with some alarm. Indeed, since about 1980, most government thinking in the OECD countries has reflected the view that the economic frontiers of the state should be rolled back. On becoming British prime minister in 1979, Margaret Thatcher signalled the start of the 'Conservative revolution' in economic policy which, with the subsequent elections of Ronald Reagan as US president and Helmut Kohl as German chancellor, quickly spread beyond the UK.

One of the tenets of this revolution was that there was a need for less, not more, government. Even today, Conservative attitudes to public expenditure hold sway in Britain: the new Labour government has devolved monetary policy to the Bank of England, adhered to the 'golden rule' of borrowing only what is necessary for investment, kept the ratio of debt to GDP prudently stable and not pursued any major redistributive policies. All of this has led the *Economist* to argue that "judged by his record so far Mr Blair is proving a pretty good Tory".[2]

The intellectual bases for this economic conservatism lie in the writings of Adam Smith and Milton Friedman. At a macro-economic level, Friedman argued that all attempts by government— through expansionary fiscal or monetary policies—to keep unemployment below its 'natural' rate would only offer a temporary palliative at the expense of long-term increases in inflation. The policy implication of this analysis was that the solution to high unemployment lay in 'supply-side' measures aimed at reducing the 'natural' rate.

At the level of micro-economics, Smith had argued that an 'invisible hand' brought order and consistency to the seeming chaos of the multitude of individual actions. It is this invisible hand which today's economists and policy-makers term the 'market' and the thrust of economic theory, of the textbook variety, has been to show that, under certain conditions, market outcomes are 'efficient'. The institutional backdrop for realising this efficiency is competitive markets. The appropriate micro-economic role for government, therefore, is to remove barriers to competition. At a practical level this has meant transferring—through denationalisation, deregulation and contracting out—responsibility for several economic functions from the public to the private sector.

A rise in the proportion of GDP accounted for by government expenditure will be inevitable if growth of the latter outstrips that of the former. Even if real government expenditure and real GDP grew at the same rate, however, differential productivity growth between the public and private sectors would ensure that, in nominal terms, government expenditure as a proportion of GDP would rise. This 'relative price effect' occurs because while rising productivity gains, to some extent, offset the increasing cost of labour in the private sector it is conventionally assumed that there are no such gains associated with the public provision of goods and services.

There is, of course, nothing inevitable about such a rise: it relies on wage-growth parity between public- and private-sector workers. Nor is it inevitable that productivity growth in public goods and services must always be zero: the conventional wisdom is based on studies conducted in the 60s and 70s.

On the face of it, very little changed in the UK public sector over the 80s: it employed 5.4 million people at the beginning of the decade and about 5.2 million at its end. But there was considerable change in attitudes to work practices, whereby "choice, standards and quality [were now] the catchwords; flexibility, performance and local management the tools; the private sector the model".[3] These changes were particularly marked in four areas: pay determination, performance incentives, flexible working practices and local management.

Moreover, the setting of objectives and targets, allied to the devolution of management responsibilities, became widespread in the public sector. Indeed, the major innovation in the public sector in a number of OECD countries has been this 'new public management'. NPM attempts to improve the efficiency of public-sector organisations by applying private-sector principles of management;

these emphasise competition between decentralised units and maximum outsourcing of activities. Taken together, these changes imply that the basic assumption underlying the relative price effect—that productivity in the public sector grows more slowly than in the private, but that wages grow at the same rate—should, in the changed climate of the past decade, be treated with some caution.

Another set of explanations for the growth of public expenditure comes from public-choice theorists. They argue that government, like any other economic agent, pursues self-interest and that the self-interest of governments leads them to increase their expenditure. First, there is the electoral interest: for example, widening of the suffrage has led to the less well-off exercising their electoral power by voting for more egalitarian policies, involving higher welfare expenditures.

Secondly, interest groups demand increases in spending on specific items and/or new spending programmes. The gain from these programmes is visible and, at least, attracts the votes of those who demand them; the loss, in terms of the higher taxes and/or borrowing required to pay for this expenditure, is less visible and more diffused, since borne more broadly as higher rates of tax or interest. This can be associated with middle- and upper-income support for higher spending. British research has shown how professional and managerial families make disproportionate use of education and health services—they are more aware of their importance and live longer than working-class families—in addition to being major suppliers of them (as doctors, teachers and so on).[4]

Thirdly, the prestige of ministers and civil servants is intimately connected to the resources they garner for spending programmes within their departmental brief. As Ferdinand Mount has observed, "Bureaucrats cannot help becoming rent-seekers, in just the same way that entrepreneurs cannot help becoming profit-maximisers. It is their occupational deformation to regard the size, financial resources and morale of their department as intimately connected with the public good."[5]

Growth in public expenditure has been concentrated in the three big social programmes: social security benefits (including pensions), health and education. Since expenditure on these items is related to exogenous influences—demography and the state of the economic cycle—there has been a sense of helplessness on the part of governments in the face of ever-expanding public-spending figures.

The main force behind this expansion has been an ageing population. In every OECD country the 'support ratio'—working-age individuals divided by those over 65—is predicted steadily to decline. In the UK it is likely to fall from 4.2 in 1980 to 3.1 by 2040.

This has two implications. First, there is upward pressure on health-care costs: average costs for over-75s are nine times as great, and for those between 65 and 75 four times as great, as for individuals of working age.

Secondly, under a pay-as-you-go pension scheme—where each generation effectively pays the pensions of the preceding one—proportionately fewer employees meeting the pension needs of retirees may require rising public-expenditure commitment. Labour-market trends, particularly the higher participation of women, have also had profound consequences, inflating the number of prospective pensioners.

Demography also plays an important role in education expenditure—this time reducing the pressure for spending on compulsory schooling, via falling fertility rates in most OECD countries. But this factor has been offset by increased participation in post-compulsory education, associated with rising educational qualifications—reflecting a realisation by governments that improved education and training are essential for industrial competitiveness. Thus, overall, real spending per student has continued to grow.

Lastly, the state of the economy has itself a major influence upon social-security expenditure. This goes beyond the payment of benefits to the unemployed. In the UK, and especially in Northern Ireland, aggravating the problem of unemployment is labour-market inactivity: the fastest growing component of the social-security budget in the past 15 years has been invalidity benefit.

In sum, therefore, much of the growth in public expenditure in OECD countries might be explained by demographic and social factors, generating a 'demand' for certain types of expenditure (both final and transfer). The sources of this demand lie in increasing claimants and a desire for higher standards of provision. Overlying this trend are cyclical movements linked to economic depression. In democratic societies, public-expenditure decisions, however benignly motivated, cannot be separated from what the public wants: governments choose to meet demand because, in large part, it is in their political interest to do so.

But these trends, if unchecked, would have meant that by this decade in some countries public expenditure would have accounted for more than three quarters of GDP. That this did not come to pass was due to mounting fiscal crisis, as voters became increasingly averse to funding the increases in taxation rising expenditure demands required.

The revolt of the tax-payers provided the catalyst for a dramatic reversal of attitudes towards public expenditure: instead of being seen as an instrument of good, as it had been from 1945 to 1974, it came to be seen in the 80s and the 90s as a harmful economic influence. Politicians in several countries have since campaigned on the promise of 'no new taxes'. Labour's defeat in the British general election of 1992 was widely ascribed to its proposal to put up marginal tax rates; Tony Blair was (and remains) desperate to convince the electorate that it need not fear taxes going up under new Labour.

In other words, there has been a dramatic change in the market for votes. As Tyrie observes, the median voter is likely to be a white-collar home-owner who is aware of, and anxious about, his tax burden.[6] All parties are fearful of being branded as high-tax and the question 'where will the money come from?', which inevitably greets any policy proposal that involves new monies, has made parties circumspect about what can be achieved through the public purse.

Changes in the political market-place have brought changes in the rhetoric of politics. Gone is the vision of the Great Society, where wise and generous public spending would be the rising tide that lifted all boats. In its place is a society which 'understands less and blames more'. The welfare state is charged with creating incentives which lead to social pathologies: single motherhood, weak labour-force attachment and crime are due to a state which rewards, or does not adequately punish, deviant behaviour, it is said; high tax rates and state encroachment in the economy sap incentives and enterprise and make for inefficiencies.

Current intellectual fashion plays down the role of the state in promoting good economic performance. Instead, attitudes towards government spending are couched in terms of 'restraint' and 'priorities'. Even if 'rolling back the frontiers of the state' may be too extreme for some, expanding these frontiers appears undesirable to all.

In response to the fiscal crisis wrought by growing public expenditure, governments have taken action on three broad fronts:
• reduction in the scale of state activity through cuts in public expenditure;
• reduction in the scope of state activity through privatisation and contracting out; and
• improvements in the efficiency of state activity through NPM.

Achieving significant, real cuts in public expenditure is extremely difficult. In the UK, nearly half of all expenditure consists of transfer payments made in response to demographic (old-age) and economic (unemployment) contingencies. That part spent on publicly-provided goods and services is constrained by party commitments ('the National Health Service is safe in our hands') or susceptible to threats of industrial action by powerful public-sector unions. As a consequence, such public-expenditure cuts as are attempted fall on the less visible parts of the budget, which usually means capital expenditure.

Nevertheless, major changes have been attempted. Linking state pensions to prices rather than wages, and equalising the state pension age at 65 for men and women, has saved about £8 billion. Non-pension transfers have been pruned through rule-tightening—such as reduction of the duration of what was unemployment benefit from 12 to six months—and bearing down on benefit fraud.

As regards public-sector pay, the monolithic structure of wage negotiations has been broken down—for both occupations and regions. For example, teachers, dentists, doctors, nurses, paramedics and senior civil servants are all subject to independent pay reviews. Meanwhile, performance-related pay is spreading downwards from senior management.

A start has also been made on zero-based budgeting. Every few years, each spending department in the UK undertakes a root-and-branch review to see if its spending programmes are still needed and, of those that are, whether they could be delivered more efficiently.

In 1992 alone, across the world, $69 billion worth of state-owned firms passed into private hands and, if planned privatisations materialise, this figure could double by 2002. Indeed, a policy which, in 1983, appeared heretical to all but the most radical believer in free markets is today conventional wisdom.

Privatisation policies were pioneered in the UK and pursued so vigorously by the successive Conservative governments elected from 1979 that there is little left to sell. Today, every public utility in England is privatised—British Telecom in 1984, gas in 1986, water in 1989, electricity in 1990—and the government has divested itself of ownership in several areas of industry. By 1996, the proportion of GDP resulting from the activities of publicly-owned enterprises had fallen to just 2 per cent.

But this was by no means only a British fashion. The French privatisation programme, legislation for which was passed in June 1993, expects revenues of $50 billion through the privatisation of 21 state-owned firms. The Italian government hopes to raise $10-15 billion through its privatisation programme.

In the past five years, however, the centre-stage for privatisation has shifted from Europe to Latin America: in 1992, this region accounted for 35 per cent (compared with only 6 per cent in 1988) of the total value of privatisations in the world. Even this may be dwarfed by privatisation in eastern Europe and the countries of the former Soviet Union: in 1992, with its privatisation programme still not fully under way, this region accounted for 32 per cent of the total world value of privatisations.

A further reduction in the role of the state has come from the contracting out of functions previously performed within the public sector: cleaning, catering, security and so on. Of course, from a social point of view, privatisation and contracting out offer no advantages (in terms of resource savings) unless accompanied by greater efficiency and without dilution of the quality of the product.

Vickers and Yarrow have argued[7] that when privatisation was applied in the UK to industries in reasonably competitive markets, the policy was a success. It was, however, less successful when applied to firms with monopoly power. First, the obstacles to entry into these industries continued even after privatisation. Secondly, problems of access by the regulator to good-quality information meant that the regulated firms had considerable influence on the formula governing their prices. Thirdly, the focus of regulation has been entirely on price and has ignored regulatory incentives for investment behaviour—a point with particular force for the water industry, given the expensive investment needed to bring water and sewerage standards up to EU environmental requirements.

A basic rationale for government intervention in the economy remains, however— the notion of market failure, recently extended to embrace the process of economic development. Interest in the role of government as a catalyst for economic growth is derived from the observation that in most of the world's most successful economies governments have played an active role in guiding the course of economic development.

It has been argued that the development task facing countries today is different from a century ago. Then it was one of invention and innovation; today it is imitation and adaptation. This requires committing current resources to producing future and uncertain output. The risk is of otherwise missing potential markets and it is this which provides the basis for, and direction of, government intervention.

The creation of 'future-oriented' institutions is particularly important in manufacturing. This stems from the nature of modern industry, with its requirements of large-scale investment, specialised and lengthy training for managers and workers, competitively priced inputs and access to foreign markets.

Investment requires financial institutions that will lend long-term at competitive interest. Training needs government underwriting to overcome fears by firms that their training expenditure will be wasted if trained workers are poached by others. Competitively priced inputs require wage-negotiation machinery such that pay does not grow faster than productivity—as may happen under 'free collective bargaining'. And access to markets requires that the exchange rate be kept low and stable.

The role of state intervention in the economy is one of the oldest debates in economics. It revolves around three questions: when, where and how much to intervene. It is recognised, however, that it is the quality, not the quantity, of intervention that is important. It is differences in quality that explain why large-scale state intervention has proved disastrous in Latin America and in the

**Setting priorities will not be easy**

erstwhile countries of the Soviet bloc, yet so successful in Japan, Taiwan and Korea—prior to the recent global travails which have hit both sets of countries indiscriminately.

In Northern Ireland, high rates of unemployment—with over half the unemployed long-term unemployed—mean that market failure is most starkly revealed in the difficulties the unemployed have in finding jobs. A major risk the Northern Ireland economy faces, therefore, is that a significant proportion of its population remains socially excluded.

The terminology of 'work-poor' households, in which there are no earners—as against the 'work-rich' households, which have more than one—has already entered the vocabulary of politicians. In the UK, the proportion of work-poor households increased from 6.5 per cent in 1975 to 18.5 per cent in 1994; meanwhile, the proportion of work-rich rose, more marginally, from 56 to 60 per cent.

As joblessness has become concentrated in particular families, so has income inequality between households grown—a problem exacerbated by widening individual inequality between skilled and unskilled among those in work, and by the concentration of poor families in particular neighbourhoods and housing estates. The socially excluded lack (or, at least, do not display) the social and cultural skills, and values, of mainstream working-class and middle-class people and may adopt a life-style 'normal' society would regard as 'undesirable'. The low incomes associated with unemployment or unskilled employment increase the attractiveness of illegal and even criminal activities.

Moreover, unemployment reduces the 'marriageability' of young men. Men who cannot support a family are unlikely to form one, while women who can support themselves—and any children they might have—find that being single "shields them from the type of exploitation that often accompanies the sharing of limited resources".[8] Indeed, while unemployment amongst unskilled men has risen, the rise in women's employment—coupled with the fact that a woman is often better off as a lone parent than living with an unemployed man—means women have less need for economic support from men today than they did, say, 20 years ago. Result: many men can't marry, many women won't marry.

Furthermore, social exclusion may itself enhance the problems of male joblessness, as persistent poverty and chronic unemployment express themselves in 'perverse' behaviours inappropriate to entering the labour market, with its requirements of self-discipline and self-respect.

There is no single criterion by which people are socially excluded. Unemployment may exclude an individual from the world of work. Poverty (often, but not necessarily, a consequence of unemployment) may exclude a person from the world of consumption and social intercourse. And these facets have effects, perhaps conflicting: a single parent included in the world of work under threat of loss of benefit may still feel excluded from the domain of the family.

All in all, it is in the arena of social exclusion that public expenditure, and the energies of policy-makers and their advisors, need most to be directed.[9] ∎

**Footnotes**

[1] This paper was written while I was a visiting fellow at the Policy Institute, Trinity College, Dublin and I am grateful to the institute and the college for providing me with research facilities.

[2] *Economist*, May 2nd 1998

[3] See Andrew Adonis' related series of articles in the *Financial Times*, July-August 1991.

[4] J Le Grand and D Winter, 'The middle classes and the welfare state under Conservative and Labour governments', *Journal of Public Policy*, vol 6, 1987, pp 399-430

[5] F Mount, *The British Constitution Now*, Mandarin, London, 1992

[6] A Tyrie, *The Prospects for Public Spending*, Social Market Foundation, London, 1996

[7] J Vickers and G Yarrow, *Privatization: An Economic Analysis*, MIT Press, Cambridge, Mass, 1989

[8] W J Wilson, *When Work Disappears*, Albert A Knopf, New York, 1996

[9] A raft of detailed policy proposals is contained in *Social Exclusion, Social Inclusion*, Democratic Dialogue report 2, Belfast, 1995.

# Public expenditure on the eve of devolution

**Richard Barnett
Graeme Hutchinson**[1]

In terms of constitutional issues, the Labour government at Westminster promises to be one of the great reforming administrations of the century. Democratically elected regional governments are being introduced in Northern Ireland, Scotland and Wales and regional levels of governance are to be considered in England where demand is sufficient.

The government is not operating according to a blueprint: an *à la carte* approach is being taken, the precise structure of the regional bodies varying to meet perceived circumstances. The form of government to operate in Northern Ireland is set out in the Good Friday agreement.[2]

A key issue for the overall governance of the United Kingdom is the achievement of UK-wide priorities in the context of substantive regional decision-making.

With the increasing importance of trans-border economic relations and growing demand for regional government, it is recognised worldwide that many national governments are 'too big for the small things' and 'too small for the big things'. Yet, as it develops a system of regional governance, it is not clear that the Labour government has recognised this new reality and what it means for priority-setting.

One indication that central government is not yet sufficiently attuned to the impending political realities of devolution is provided by the government's terms of reference for the comprehensive spending review in Scotland, which affirm: "One of the main objectives of the review … will be to hand over to the Parliament an overall public expenditure programme that is already effective and properly focused on Scotland's needs." Is it not for Scotland's Parliament to determine what Scotland needs? And ditto for Northern

Ireland's Assembly?

Within the annual Public Expenditure Survey (PES)—to date, the focus of all expenditure decision-making in the UK—Northern Ireland public expenditure is allocated by a block-formula system. While the origin of this formula can be traced to the late 70s, the history of apportioning public expenditure within the UK on a formula basis is more extensive.

For instance, the Goschen formula (named after George Goschen, chancellor of the exchequer in Lord Salisbury's 1886-92 administration) was the mechanism whereby Scotland received 11/80ths of British spending on comparable programmes. The proportion was based on the assignment of probate duties relative to exchequer contributions.[3] It fell into abeyance after the second world war.

Similarly, in Northern Ireland during devolution, there were various arrangements—particularly with regard to social services—for allocating funds using broad population formulae.[4] During the 60s and 70s, public-expenditure plans for UK regions were however settled collectively by negotiation within the wider PES, rather than by formulae.

It was not until the late 70s, when devolution to Scotland and Wales seemed imminent, that a population-based formula returned to the political agenda. Its author was Joel Barnett, chief secretary to the Treasury in the 1974-79 Labour government, and the 'Barnett formula'—established in 1978 before the abortive Scottish and Welsh referenda—remains in operation today. Twenty years on, its future should be discussed, especially in the context of renewed devolutionary developments.

For purposes of planning and consistency, Northern Ireland—as with Scotland and Wales—is treated as a single block within the annual PES. Although the respective secretaries of state have discretion to switch funds within their block, it must be consistent with overall government policy.

In theory, the Northern Ireland secretary has had the greatest discretion, since the block allocates almost all programme expenditure in the region—98 per cent in 1995-96—with only expenditure by the regional agricultural department on 'national' agricultural and fisheries support excluded.

As Thain and Wright observe, this vastly overestimates the true extent of discretion once the 'parity principle' is accepted, since social security is only nominally within the block:[5] the managed block thus comprised 63 per cent of programme expenditure in Northern Ireland in 1995-96. Yet in Scotland and Wales, items not encompassed in their respective blocks—over and above social security—include all expenditure on agriculture, fisheries and food and on industry, energy and employment.

The Barnett formula, based on the population balance between England, Scotland and Wales (85:10:5), allocated any *changes* in planned public expenditure between them—it was never envisaged that the formula would allocate *levels* of expenditure. Similar arrangements were agreed for Northern Ireland, although its formula is based on the region's share of the UK population, rather than that of Great Britain.

The formula only applies to expenditure *within* the blocks; non-block expenditure is determined through conventional bidding. Thus, as David Heald argues,[6] there are two components to block expenditure:

- the inherited expenditure base, which dates back to the period when the formula was first implemented, and
- the incremental expenditure, determined by the operation of the formula.

In 1992 the formulae were subjected to their first and only revision, using new population estimates. In Northern Ireland, block expenditure is adjusted by applying a percentage of 2.87 (2.75 pre-1992) to the totality of changes in comparable programmes in Britain. While the formula adjustment reflected the 1991 census returns, Thain and Wright suggest that "of equal importance in the decision to revise it was the Chief Secretary's attempt to keep total spending in line with published targets".[7]

Over the long term, operation of the Barnett formula should bring about a convergence in public expenditure per head across UK regions/nations, as the population-based increments gradually predominated over the disparate inherited levels. Obviously, the rate of convergence would depend on public expenditure growth (the faster spending increased in England, the faster convergence would occur), as well as on the stability of population shares (relative population decline in a well-endowed region would reduce convergence).

The Barnett formula was first applied to Northern Ireland when public expenditure reductions appeared probable, not least because of the relatively high baseline of expenditure in the region. The attractiveness of the formula was obvious: any cuts would thereby be no worse than proportionate.[8]

Since then, however there has been some convergence down towards the UK average (Table 1). Not only has UK expenditure not fallen since the early 80s; apart from the 1992 adjustment, the fixity of the formula has worked to Northern Ireland's disbenefit as its population share has risen.[9]

But identifiable public expenditure includes the social-security programme, outside the scope of the Barnett formula. When social security is excluded, the degree of convergence is somewhat reduced. At the same time, identifiable public expenditure covers only around 75 per cent of total spending; more attention should thus be paid to assessing comparable public expenditure across the four components of the UK. Heald suggests such an exercise would reveal greater convergence[10] than the identifiable series implies.[11]

The fact that the formula has survived for so long—including its reaffirmation by the current Labour administration—would suggest it must have some beneficial (two-way) qualities. For the Treasury, the formula is simple and the need for annual negotiations between the centre and the regions/nations is avoided. The fact that it has produced "a fair and politically acceptable distribution of funds over a long period"[12] would endorse Heald's view that it is an effective mechanism of territorial management in a highly centralised state.[13] For the regions/nations, there is less scrutiny of block programmes than other spending departments endure, as well as the discretion to address self-defined priorities.

The drawbacks are administrative and/or political. The former include

**Table 1: Treasury analysis of 'identifiable' public expenditure per head (£m)**

|  | 1990-91 | 1995-96 | Change (%) | Change (exc social security) |
|---|---|---|---|---|
| United Kingdom | 2715 | 3889 | 43 | 36 |
| Northern Ireland | 3858 | 5139 | 33 | 33 |
| England | 2611 | 3743 | 43 | 36 |
| Scotland | 3204 | 4614 | 44 | 35 |
| Wales | 2957 | 4352 | 47 | 37 |

Source: HM Treasury, *Statistical Supplement* (various issues)

'formula bypass'. The regions/nations tend to benefit when additional expenditure occurring *during* a financial year—pay awards, for example—is allocated on the basis of cost rather than the formula. Since Scotland and Northern Ireland spend more *per capita* on health than England, they are likely to gain a larger share of any such additional resources than would be suggested by a strict application of the Barnett formula. And the fact that England is the base country means that clear comparators are sometimes difficult to obtain.

But the fact that the formula kept the same population relatives from its inception until the early 90s clearly benefited Scotland (where population fell) rather than Wales or Northern Ireland (where it rose), and the only viable explanation appears to be political. Had the formula been revised, Scotland would have fared less well, and this would have done little to improve the electoral prospects of the

Conservatives there, under pressure as they were from Labour and the Nationalists throughout the 80s—a problem they did not, of course, face in Northern Ireland.

Yet, though Northern Ireland was adversely affected by the formula remaining unchanged for as long as it did, the fact that the region still enjoys higher spending per head (albeit falling in relative terms) would suggest there have been real benefits from additional allocations above comparability.[14]

As to the future, the government has undertaken to update the population figures from 1999-2000 and annually thereafter.[15] The fact that it has deemed 'fair'[16] the settlements arising out of the block-formula arrangements suggests it sees little point in adjusting something that already works. There have, however, been calls for modifications.

Most notably, Lord Barnett himself, in evidence to the Treasury Select Committee, has advocated a formula that takes account of rising income per head in the regions/nations of the UK, as well as needs and expenditure—Barnett mark II. The current formula takes no account of spending needs, beyond population.

In the interests of fiscal rectitude, there may be arguments in favour of conducting a needs-assessment exercise similar to that carried out by the Treasury in the late 70s.[17] Such an exercise would seek to determine the appropriateness of the Barnett formula—how it relates to need and how total expenditure (not just marginal changes) has been allocated according to need. As we argue below, however, one problem with this type of analysis is that assessment of need is highly subjective.[18]

While Lord Barnett has advocated revisions to the formula, he continues to support its underlying principles. He told the Treasury Select Committee: "I am flattered that the Barnett formula has lasted twenty years. I hope it will last much longer. At the time, I must confess, I did not think it would last a year or even twenty minutes."[19]

But despite the formula's longevity, it has never been tested in the environment for which it was designed—devolved government. While regional decision-makers (the secretaries of state and their ministerial teams) have had discretion to vary policy, they have always had overarching policy objectives in line with those of the UK-wide government of which they have been members. With devolved government, this congruence of overarching goals may cease. Indeed, one of the prime objectives of devolution is reflection of regional preference in policy decisions.

A key aspect of the economics of multi-level government, or 'fiscal federalism', is the assignment problem. This refers to the allocation of functions between different levels of government—the who-should-do-what? question. It is conventional to divide the economic functions of government into macro-economic stabilisation, income (and wealth) redistribution and the efficient allocation of resources (correction of micro-economic market failures). The widely held consensus is that the macro-economic and redistributive functions should be allocated to the higher level of government.

In splitting the micro-economic function between the various levels, the key factor is the geographic area over which the benefits of the policy extend. In the case of public goods, for example, some are 'national' in scope while others are more regional. The 'decentralisation theorem' shows that welfare increases if provision reflects the preferences of those who benefit from the good or service. Since 'national' governments tend to provide services uniformly, it follows that regional determination of provision is likely to be welfare-enhancing.

But if resources are allocated, via the Barnett formula, in an environment in which some public spending reflects regional policy priorities, accountability will be blurred. Regional government will always be able to blame central government when it fails to provide services to a high standard. Bloomfield and Carter warn that it may "spend its time complaining about the parsimony of the Treasury".[20] Such a lack of clear lines of accountability and the resultant squabbling over who is to blame is already evident in local government in England, where extensive rate-capping has left local politicians allocating public-service funds from an essentially fixed budget.

Bloomfield and Carter's solution is for regional government to have tax-raising powers, and in terms of accountable government this makes perfect sense: accountability implies that the government that spends money should be accountable to its electorate by having to raise taxes to pay for public programmes. But it is important to distinguish between marginal and full accountability.[21]

Full accountability would require that the regional assembly raised all its funds from regional sources of taxation, and this is not feasible. Fiscal imbalance is a characteristic of almost all multi-level governments. Typically, the higher level of government is assigned tax-raising powers in excess of its expenditure needs, while the reverse is the case for lower levels.

There is, however, a strong case for building marginal accountability into the public-finance structure for a regional assembly. Without such marginal accountability, there is no clear designation of responsibility for public-spending decisions.

Under the proposed Northern Ireland arrangements, the only tax under the control of the Assembly will be the regional rate. This is used to help fund those services, such as primary and secondary education, which are local government responsibilities in Britain but are currently the responsibility of central departments in Northern Ireland. With the regional rate as the only 'safety valve' providing flexibility for the Assembly budget, there is a danger it will be used inappropriately. Also, it is not a tax which is readily associated in the minds of the electorate with services not provided by local government. A regional income tax would seem a more appropriate tax for the Assembly.[22]

The arguments against allocating some tax-raising power to a regional assembly are neither strong nor convincing. First, it is argued that central government has a responsibility for achieving macro-economic stability and that the public sector borrowing requirement is a key policy instrument in this regard. (This was one of the arguments used for restricting the expenditure and tax-raising ability of local authorities in Britain.) But additions to expenditure financed out of regional taxes have no impact on the PSBR.

More broadly, it is argued that central government has a policy objective to control public spending. While such an objective might be defended—on the assertion that public expenditure 'crowds out' private investment—central government must recognise that in the new policy environment of devolved governance some aspects of control will be lost. There is a cost-benefit calculation here: the benefits of effective and accountable devolved government easily outweigh the costs of some loss of overall control of public expenditure.

The blurring of accountability which will result from application of the Barnett formula in the new context is a consequence of a system of funding for regional government which relies to all intents and purposes wholly on block-grant transfer from central government. Other weaknesses of the precise form of the block grant generated by the formula might also emerge.

Most systems of intergovernmental transfers would take cognisance of access to regional taxes (differential *resources*) and expenditure *needs*. That differential tax-base resources have not been an issue in discussion of the Barnett formula is purely because it gives no role for regional taxation. Nevertheless, any system of intergovernmental transfers should be transparent and simple to understand. Given the relatively small role that regional taxation is likely to play in the overall regional budget, even with tax-raising powers, we do not believe any differentials in regional tax bases should be a concern.

Furthermore, attempts to correct for differential tax-base resources generally require matching grants from central government. Such funding does have PSBR implications: the greater is regional spending, the greater will be the centre's obligation to pay grant. As a consequence, it is likely to be resisted by central government.

In the existing Barnett formula, population is taken to be an (or, more precisely, the) indicator of expenditure need. Lord Barnett believes that the indicator should be revised, albeit modestly. We would caution against any movement towards a comprehensive needs assessment, for two inter-related reasons.

First, as Midwinter highlighted in his evidence to the Treasury Select Committee, there is no objective measure of expenditure need.[23] Ultimately, needs assessment is a political exercise.

Secondly, comprehensive needs assessments tend to result in complicated formulae which lack transparency. It is always easy, then, for central government to adjust the various weights used in the needs-assessment model to achieve its own political objectives—the model used for allocating funds to British local authorities provides ample evidence for this. Also, to aid accountability, it is desirable that the total quantities of the intergovernmental transfer should not vary significantly, year-on-year. A simple formula, with limited scope for central manipulation, is most likely to produce such stability.

Discussions of the public sector in Northern Ireland almost always include some mention of the so-called subvention—the difference between public spending in the region and taxes raised. Any such discussion needs to be more broadly based than often in the past, for two main reasons.

First, such calculations are always incomplete. For example, the package of economic measures for Northern Ireland[24] announced by the chancellor, Gordon Brown, in May included some £100 million of tax expenditures. Tax expenditures represent an important part of the overall fiscal system, yet rarely is any attempt made to include them in calculations of subventions to the various regions/nations of the UK. Their inclusion would be likely to alter radically the pattern of regional subventions, but arriving at an agreed measure is impossible, since there is no obvious counterfactual to use as a baseline in the calculations.[25]

Secondly, subventions to various regions of a state are a typical feature of devolved systems of government. By international standards the size of the subventions to the various components of the UK, including Northern Ireland, is perhaps not atypical.[26]

The concept of society within which devolution is to take place is also relevant. One model, favoured by some economists, is competitive regionalism or 'Balkanisation'[27]—in which the country is little more than a collection of regions and, unless families and other factors are perfectly mobile, living standards and public services may vary considerably between regions, depending on their ability to compete. In such a framework the subvention—as indeed most, if not all, fiscal transfers—is viewed negatively.

We do not believe this is the context within which devolution is being introduced in the UK. Society is something more than a collection of regions, families are not perfectly mobile and should not be forced to move, and living standards are a UK-wide concern. In this framework, social goals may dominate purely economic ones. Thus, while in narrow economic terms a large subvention (appropriately measured to allow for tax expenditures) may cause a deadweight loss,[28] this must be set against the broader social benefits any subvention helps achieve.

Yet there are clearly aspects of Northern Ireland's large public sector which hinder regional economic performance—for example, the high public-private wage differential.[29] Any such detrimental factors should, however, be addressed directly, with any impact on the subvention following as a consequence.

Having explored the mechanism determining the public expenditure available to the Northern Ireland secretary—the block-formula system—the next question is the means by which this is apportioned between government departments and how these departments express their requirements.

In Northern Ireland the public expenditure 'programme total' includes

**Table 2: public expenditure in Northern Ireland, 1979-80 to 1995-96**

| Period | Change at constant prices (%) | Change as proportion of GDP (%) |
| --- | --- | --- |
| 1979-80 to 1982-83 | -6.7 | 2.2 |
| 1982-83 to 1986-87 | 3.7 | -7.3 |
| 1986-87 to 1990-91 | -0.9 | -5.4 |
| 1990-91 to 1995-96 | 15.1 | 0.7 |
| 1979-80 to 1995-96 | 10.3 | -9.8 |

Source: *Northern Ireland Expenditure Plans and Priorities* (various issues)

central government expenditure, grants to district councils and the external financing of public corporations. Items not included relate to those UK departments that provide services in Northern Ireland (expenditure on the army and the court service).

There is no universally acceptable method of measuring the growth of public expenditure. Convention usually dictates a twofold approach: relating public expenditure to gross domestic product,[30] and expressing the cash figures in real terms. As to the latter, the 'deflator' used to correct for inflation should take account of the public-sector environment. Thus, instead of using the common GDP price deflator, we adopt an index of the prices of those goods and services purchased by the public sector in the UK.[31]

The figures presented in Table 2 illustrate the growth in public expenditure between 1979-80 and 1995-96, both when converted to constant prices (1990) and as a proportion of GDP. The dramatic growth in public expenditure in Northern Ireland has frequently been remarked upon, but this was very much a phenomenon of the 70s.

Public expenditure has continued to grow subsequently—10 per cent in real terms in the period under review, or an annual growth of 0.6 per cent. But growth has been particularly associated with

Table 3: public expenditure change per annum in real terms, by economic category (%)

| Category | 1984-1988 | 1988-1992 | 1992-1995 | 1984-1995 |
|---|---|---|---|---|
| Departmental running costs (net of receipts) | 1.3 | 3.7 | -2.1 | 1.4 |
| Other public service pay and other expenditure on goods and services | 2.0 | 0.7 | 2.1 | 1.9 |
| Subsidies | -6.3 | -2.9 | 3.8 | -2.8 |
| Current grants | 0.8 | 3.9 | 3.0 | 3.3 |
| Net capital expenditure on assets | 2.9 | 5.4 | -2.5 | 2.6 |
| Capital grants | -4.7 | -6.4 | -3.6 | -4.6 |
| Lending and other financial transactions | 21.7 | -17.5 | -3.2 | -6.4 |
| Total | 1.4 | 0.02 | 1.7 | 1.3 |

Source: *Northern Ireland Expenditure Plans and Priorities* (various issues)

recession, as in 1990-91 to 1992-93, when real growth was almost 8 per cent. And there has been a clear *decline* in the ratio to GDP—from 68.9 to 59.1 per cent.[32] This finding is consistent with international experience[33] which, as Oxley and Martin argue,[34] reflects concerns about the impact of continuing public-sector expansion on private-sector performance and greater appreciation of the social costs of higher taxation.

Table 3 decomposes public expenditure by economic category for selected years between 1984-85 and 1995-96. This provides some indication of how the public sector interacts with the rest of the economy. The first two components of the table—departmental running costs and other public-service pay—can broadly be taken to indicate the contribution public-sector employment has had to public spending.

The sum of these categories increased in real terms over the period by 22 per cent, or 1.9 per cent annually—again much less than in the 70s.[35] Public-sector employment grew by 40 per cent between 1970 and 1974, and by a further 25 per cent between 1974 and 1979,[36] but thereafter steadily declined.

The subsidy and capital-grant components of Table 3 also fell substantially over the period (by 33 and 55 per cent respectively), highlighting the growing reticence of government to provide wholesale fiscal support to the private sector. Policy documents such as *Pathfinder* and *Competing in the 1990s*[37] reflected the concern of government that heavy reliance on public funds by many companies was insulating them from competition and thus hindering innovation and growth.

By contrast, there has been significant growth in current grants, overwhelmingly social-security benefits (82 per cent in 1995-96), increasing by 39 per cent over the period. This is again consistent with international experience, in that income redistribution appears to have been the core activity of most governments in recent decades.[38] The erratic behaviour of the component covering lending and other financial transactions may be explained by the fact that in 1988-89 (and 1989-90) it was enlarged to cover the payments made by the Industrial Development Board on behalf of the government for the privatisation of Short Brothers and Harland and Wolff.

The fact that definitions of public expenditure in Northern Ireland have been periodically revised (as in the rest of the UK) indicates the problems associated with its control—in the sense of establishing budgetary procedures to ensure chosen objectives are secured. The introduction of the planning total meant that grants to district councils, but not local-government expenditure financed from the rates, were included—the justification being that public expenditure should relate only to those areas where central government has control.[39] In 1992 the 'new control total' was introduced, removing the cyclical element of social-security expenditure which had been extremely difficult to predict.

One way of determining how effectively public expenditure is controlled is to compare projected to actual out-turns (Table 4). Actual public expenditure in Northern Ireland exceeded its estimated total six times between 1983-84 and 1995-96. (For purposes of continuity, the cyclical social-security component is included throughout, although the figures in brackets in the last three rows represent the difference between the actual and estimated control total.)

But there were seven occasions between 1983-84 and 1993-94 when the out-turn for UK public expenditure as a whole exceeded the plan[40]—indeed, the scale of the overspend was higher than for Northern Ireland specifically, except in 1988-89 when the overspend in the region was due to the privatisation issues. So the procedures for allocating public spending in the region do appear to represent an effective mechanism for territorial management. The separate treatment of cyclical social-security benefits from 1993-94 would suggest that the new control total represents a marginal improvement in the control process.

The process of priority-setting in Northern Ireland is much the same as in the rest of the UK: the central tenet has been, to date, the annual PES. Decisions are made in the autumn on cash plans for the year ahead, with more flexible plans for the following two years. As these figures comprise the base for subsequent surveys, it is not surprising that the most important factor in the size and composition of the budget is the previous year's version.

Recent announcements may, however, change this. In the *Treasury's Economic and Fiscal Strategy Report*,[41] which set the framework for the results of the Comprehensive Spending Review (see below),

**Table 4: Northern Ireland public expenditure, estimated and actual out-turns**

|  | Estimated out-turn (£bn) | Out-turn (£bn) | Difference (£bn) | Difference (%) |
|---|---|---|---|---|
| 1983-84 | 3.806 | 3.816 | 0.01 | 0.3 |
| 1984-85 | 4.059 | 4.064 | 0.005 | 0.1 |
| 1985-86 | 4.270 | 4.303 | 0.033 | 0.8 |
| 1986-87 | 4.663 | 4.534 | -0.129 | -2.8 |
| 1987-88 | 4.910 | 4.860 | -0.05 | -1.0 |
| 1988-89 | 5.198 | 5.465 | 0.267 | 5.1 |
| 1989-90 | 5.780 | 5.749 | -0.031 | -0.5 |
| 1990-91 | 5.912 | 5.899 | -0.013 | -0.2 |
| 1991-92 | 6.449 | 6.471 | 0.022 | 0.3 |
| 1992-93 | 7.092 | 7.084 | -0.008 | -0.1 |
| 1993-94 | 7.595 (7.109) | 7.624 (7.104) | 0.029 (-0.005) | 0.4 (-0.1) |
| 1994-95 | 8.054 (7.492) | 7.961 (7.416) | -0.093 (-0.076) | -1.2 (-1.0) |
| 1995-96 | 8.387 (7.823) | 8.259 (7.714) | -0.128 (-0.109) | -1.5 (-1.4) |

Source: *Northern Ireland Expenditure Plans and Priorities* (various issues)

cash plans are to be made for three years in advance, precisely with the aim to move away from the short-term, incremental procedures characteristic of the annual spending round.

As things stand, the Department of Finance and Personnel, which acts as the manager of the block programme, initially forwards guidelines to the Northern Ireland departments and the Northern Ireland Office, seeking information on public spending in the region relative to the rest of the UK—as Thain and Wright put it, "comparability provides the bedrock of territorial expenditure".[42] When the DFP receives PES returns from the departments and the NIO, these are scrutinised and revised during the

Table 5: real public expenditure growth per annum, 1979-80 to 1995-96, by function (%)

| Function | 1979-1982 | 1982-1986 | 1986-1990 | 1990-1995 | 1979-1995 |
|---|---|---|---|---|---|
| Agriculture* | -5.4 | 0.4 | -1.1 | 3.3 | -0.6 |
| Industry, energy, trade and employment | -8.5 | -3.4 | -3.6 | -1.3 | -3.4 |
| Transport and roads | -8.7 | -1.5 | -2.0 | -0.8 | -2.8 |
| Housing | -2.8 | -0.9 | -8.8 | -2.9 | -3.6 |
| Environment | -1.4 | -2.3 | 2.1 | -4.0 | -1.7 |
| Law and order** | -0.8 | 2.1 | 1.2 | 2.4 | 1.8 |
| Education, science, arts and libraries | -2.2 | 1.1 | 2.1 | 1.8 | 1.0 |
| Health and social services | 0.7 | 0.6 | 1.4 | 3.1 | 2.0 |
| Social security | 2.9 | 3.0 | -0.2 | 5.2 | 3.9 |

* includes expenditure in Northern Ireland by the UK Ministry of Agriculture, Fisheries and Food
** includes expenditure by the NIO

Source: *Northern Ireland Expenditure Plans and Priorities* (various issues)

summer.

A co-ordinating committee comprising departmental and NIO permanent secretaries advises the secretary of state on negotiations with the Treasury, although the DFP view normally take precedence. Throughout the survey, the strategic priorities of public expenditure provide the baseline against which departmental proposals are considered.

Table 5 highlights the main components of public expenditure in Northern Ireland and how these have altered between 1979-80 and 1995-96, giving some indication of changing priorities. Those experiencing growth include 'law and order' (1.8 per cent per annum), health (2.0 per cent per annum) and education (1.0 per cent per annum). Their combined real growth has been 1.6 per cent per annum over the period and together they accounted for 47 per cent of public spending at its conclusion.

Those services that have experienced a real reduction over the period include industry/employment (-57.8 per cent, or -3.4 per cent per annum), housing, transport/roads and agriculture. One area of concern is that the social-security programme, which offers little in public-service provision, experienced the largest growth (3.9 per cent per annum)—in the last year of analysis (1995-96) comprising almost 36 per cent of the public expenditure budget. There can be little doubt that large and persistent unemployment and economic inactivity in the region is the main reason for this.

The trends observed in Table 5 would broadly support official claims that the priorities for public spending are mostly located within the social arena. For example, the increases in the 'law and order', education and health components are consistent with the aims of providing a stable and secure society, achieving sustained economic growth through improved educational standards, and enhancing the quality of life through general health improvement. Below these priorities, there have been several additions such as 'targeting social need' and 'policy appraisal and fair treatment'.

TSN, introduced in 1991, seeks to

address disadvantage and employment inequality. Since that entails redressing the balance between the Catholic and Protestant communities, it represents an attempt to ease intercommunal conflict and, eventually, reduce the 'law and order' programme. One problem has been the difficulty in determining those areas to which it is applicable: the Standing Advisory Commission on Human Rights highlighted (and rejected) an official view that most government expenditure, by its nature, targets social need.[43] Any process of public-expenditure priority-setting thus needs to be specific and well defined.

PAFT, introduced in 1994, seeks to ensure that all sections of the community enjoy equal opportunities and fair treatment. Aside from experiencing similar problems to TSN, the enforcement of PAFT has been particularly difficult. SACHR argued that this stemmed from insufficient status being given to the PAFT guidelines, which have enjoyed little weight in the decision-making process. A successful programme of priority-setting must then also be enforceable, preferably through statutory means. The white paper *Partnership for Equality*[44] broadly supported SACHR's findings and envisaged a more rigorous system of 'equality-proofing' in public policy and in decisions taken by public-sector organisations.

Given the scale of public expenditure in Northern Ireland and the complex array of priorities, and given that the secretary of state has "discretion to allocate resources within the Northern Ireland Block",[45] his or her responsibility in making an allocation between departments is, at least in theory, a large one. In 1995-96, for instance, the discretionary budget amounted to over £5.3 billion—total programme expenditure minus social security. But, as already intimated, a number of factors restrict the operation of these powers.

First, while each territory enjoys some detachment from the Treasury—particularly Northern Ireland, as it remains the only region to have experienced devolution before, and has retained many institutional features since—they still together comprise the union and thus are broadly subject to UK-wide policies. Moreover, while the secretary of state has discretion to allocate expenditure between programmes (though not between departments and the NIO unless the Treasury allows), any increase in one programme will normally be at the expense of others. Any deviation from the UK-wide agenda will thus first be agreed with the Treasury, which will ensure the deviation is neither unusual nor likely to have repercussions elsewhere.[46]

Secondly, as Table 3 highlighted, the major component of public spending in

Northern Ireland is pay, and within this there is little scope for the secretary of state to pursue an independent path: the main procedure for public-sector wage bargaining is again UK-wide. Even during devolution, where regional procedures were used for public services under the control of the regional government, various agreements were reached that ensured parity or equivalent pay and conditions with comparable groups in the public sector in Britain.[47] These close ties between the public sector in Northern Ireland and in the rest of the UK, while clearly beneficial to the employee, also restrict discretion in resource allocation.

Finally, the autonomy of the territorial departments does not reduce the need for monitoring and auditing of expenditure programmes. For instance, the ceiling which the block-formula system imposes on the territories means that a wasteful use of resources in one arena means less availability of funds elsewhere—including to finance regional initiatives. While the authority for scrutinising public expenditure ultimately rests with the Treasury, thereby reducing the discretionary power of the secretary of state, in Northern Ireland this is less so since the DFP examines all departmental expenditure except that of the NIO.

Once the budget decisions have been made for Northern Ireland, the onus for sharing out the funds to each of the competing departments rests with the DFP. With NIO expenditure[48] and total departmental running costs agreed first, the departments then bid for resources—programme and running costs—and the same co-ordinating committee that advised the secretary of state on negotiations with the Treasury advises the DFP on internal allocation.

While committing itself to the tight expenditure plans of the Conservatives for its first two years, the Labour government promised to reallocate resources towards its priorities—such as front-line services in education and health—via the Comprehensive Spending Review, introduced in June 1997 by the then chief secretary to the Treasury, Alistair Darling. Although the review sought to examine the whole of government spending, it had two sub-components: individual departmental reviews and cross-departmental reviews. Thain argues that the latter represented "an earnest attempt by a new administration to find the holy grail of interdepartmental co-ordination and policy cohesion".[49]

In Northern Ireland the review covered all programmes within the block, seeking from a zero base to determine whether each makes an effective contribution to the government's priorities. *De facto*, it represented the PES for 1997-98 since the latter was cancelled.

So that public expenditure in Northern Ireland remained within the totals set for 1997-98 and 1998-99, the review endeavoured to identify priorities which might attract additional resources and, conversely, areas where spending could be cut or eliminated. But while the secretary of state could reshape priorities if necessary, the terms of reference for Northern Ireland suggested her discretion was limited. Before any decisions were made as to regional changes, adequate regard had to be given to any conclusions emanating from the review of programmes in Britain.

Moreover, adjustments UK-wide in the scale of public expenditure would be reflected in increments/decrements in the Northern Ireland block covered by the Barnett formula. Therefore, while there can be little doubt that the review represents further evidence of the Treasury taking a less active role in co-ordination—"tilting further the balance between central control and departmental discretion towards departments"[50]—there is no compelling evidence that the review enhanced the discretionary power of the Northern Ireland secretary.

Thus it was in line with an overall statement by the chancellor, Mr Brown, that the secretary of state, Mo Mowlam, announced in July the upshot of the review for Northern Ireland. This set out a three-year projected rise in a new 'departmental expenditure limit'—replacing the control total—from a 1998-99 baseline of £5,680 million to £6,307 million in 2001-2. Alongside this, 'annually managed expenditure' (largely social-security benefits) was estimated to increase from £3,355 million to £3,796 million over the period.[51]

Ms Mowlam said she would discuss detailed allocations with the first and deputy first ministers, and the Assembly. Indeed, the Comprehensive Spending Review must be assessed in the context of devolution. While it will provide a useful input into decision-making and priority-setting by these regional/national levels of government, it will be for the new bodies themselves to set their priorities. With respect to the public services to be devolved, the current central government is in a sense an outgoing administration. While it might seek to do so, it cannot expect to 'tie the hands' of the incoming devolved governments.

It will be interesting to observe the attitude of the Northern Ireland Assembly to those public-expenditure planning changes envisaged in the recent Treasury report.[52] For instance, the framework of three-year planning, instead of the annual spending round, would imply that the Assembly would conduct a fundamental review of all spending decisions/priorities every three years rather than pursue the annual, incremental approach. The strict division of budgets between current and capital—with power to carry over surpluses year-to-year but not to make transfers between these categories—might also suggest that the Assembly would be unable to fund any portion of capital expenditure from surplus current revenues, as would have been possible previously.[53]

The incoming devolved governments will also inherit the new system of resource accounting, and asset registers are being compiled. With its focus on resources consumed in a year rather than on cash spent, such public accounting will lead to a more economically rational use of public-sector assets. The implications for the devolved territories are likely to be small—although, other things being equal, with their additional tier of government they are likely to have a larger asset base than other parts of the UK.

As Northern Ireland prepares to enter a régime of 'real politics' for the first time in almost three decades, the central administration—of what has been for a generation one of the most centralised systems of government—will meanwhile have to relinquish some areas of responsibility. This, experience suggests, will not be easy.

The central administration did not find it easy, for example, to change its culture to adjust to the Local Management of Schools initiative.[54] And in its 1988 'green budget', the Institute for Fiscal Studies pointed out that the government's commitment to improve front-line services in health and education was easier to secure for the former than the latter, since (in Britain) local authorities received a grant to deliver schooling from central government which they could allocate according to their own priorities.[55]

With devolution and funding via the Barnett formula, in future more services will be funded by such non-hypothecated grants and will be subject to regional priority-setting. It will be a great pity if, like a good parent, central government does not learn to 'let go'. But what does this mean for UK-wide manifesto commitments? Will central government adjust easily to a political environment in which it is less important? If not, we may see an attempt to sustain influence by the replacement of the block grant with hypothecated, or specific, funds.

The Northern Ireland Assembly, meanwhile, comprises elected representatives who have to all intents and purposes spent the last three decades in permanent opposition. They have not had to confront any of the hard decisions associated with priority-setting and resource allocation.

Yet there is already evidence that the electorate expects the Assembly to 'make a difference'. For example, there have been calls for the outcome of the review of acute-hospital provision to be put to one side, to allow the Assembly to make the final decision. Expectations are being raised that small hospitals might thereby be saved.

The main drivers for change in acute provision are not, however, political. They stem from the Royal Colleges, in terms of consultant led-provision and junior doctors' hours. The new political environment will not alter these extra-political drivers.[56] So how will the Assembly manage what in many areas are likely to be the unrealistic expectations of the electorate?

More generally, as indicated above, much of the public budget is spent on wages. Unless UK-wide bargaining is to be broken, the Assembly's room for manoeuvre will constrained by the pay bill.[57]

For very good reasons, some decisions in the assembly are to be taken on a cross-community basis, requiring:

**either** parallel consent, that is a majority of those members present and voting, including a majority of the unionist and nationalist designations present and voting;

**or** a weighted majority (60 per cent) of members present and voting, including at least 40 per cent of each of the nationalist and unionist designations present and voting.[58]

When set alongside the constituency interests of Assembly members and the loose systems of allegiance operating within the parties, the difficulties such a qualified-majority voting system may create for policy-making are evident.

Yet with sensitive powers (like human rights) 'reserved' to Westminster, the Assembly will not be dealing with traditionally divisive affairs. And the experience in Europe and in local government gives some hope of real policy innovation.[59] Moreover, we should bear in mind the principle of subsidiarity, which argues that decision-making should be carried out at as close to the citizen as possible—a natural consequence of devolved government.

The Assembly should set itself ambitious policy targets, especially in economic development. As described above, expenditure on education and health has enjoyed prioritisation at the expense of industry/employment and housing. In a period of peace, the former programmes should be maintained, but resources from 'law and order' ought to be directed towards encouraging private-sector activity through economic and employment programmes. For three reasons, we would concur with Sir George Quigley's view that the Assembly should set "stretching economic targets", involving partnership with the private sector.[60]

First, much private-sector activity in Northern Ireland is low-skilled and low-productivity, which does require assistance from government if it is to move on to a higher growth path. Current policy is correct in eschewing generalised subsidy, as against facilitating private-sector expansion. But with additional resources, albeit for the short-run, this process could be hastened, particularly in the light of possible increases in foreign direct investment.

Secondly, private-sector wages in Northern Ireland have lagged behind those in the public sector, the latter thus tending to be viewed as an employer of first resort. Convergence in public and private wages—for similar skill levels—would be desirable. Such convergence might be brought about by decentralised public wage-setting.[61] Alternatively—and with a view to protecting the quality of public services—convergence might be sought via a high-wage economy, in which private wages matched public wages institutionally set.

The industrial policy required for these two scenarios would be quite different. A priority for the Assembly must be to determine whether industrial policy is to be based on a high- or low-wage economy.

Thirdly, as remarked above, a large (and growing) component of public expenditure in Northern Ireland is social security. The deployment of 'peace-induced' resources towards employment programmes can thus be seen as a proactive measure to reduce what is not only the largest component of public spending but also one which offers little in the way of tangible services.

Therefore, assuming that a climate of peace subsists, and the 'law and order' budget can return to its pre-'troubles' level, the acquired resources ought to be used to reshape the *internal* priorities of Northern Ireland public expenditure. A more equitable balance between social and economic services would provide the fiscal framework for general prosperity.

There are, however, two apparent constraints. First, the agreement floated the possibility of a Department of Equality.[62] However welcome, this would require the usual (substantial) resources. The new body would compete for public funds in the same way as existing departments, but there are obvious and unanswered concerns about the priority such a department would be given, relative to others. As to, secondly, north-south bodies, however, it may be that policies and expenditure will be more concentrated on overcoming differences between the two administrations—not least in employment and wage structures[63]—rather than service provision.

Along with the other 'Celtic fringe' regions/nations of the UK, Northern Ireland places a high value on public services—a fact which perhaps the English-dominated Conservative governments of the 80s and 90s never really appreciated. Services such as education are valued in their own right, not just in utilitarian (or economic) terms. It is therefore likely that the Assembly will wish to improve regional public services, while developing ambitious industrial policies. This further supports the argument for a regional tax.

F or the first time in three decades, Northern Ireland is about to be in a position to determine its own priorities in key policy areas. The main political institutions are well mapped out, but for the Assembly to enjoy the success it deserves, the fiscal environment within which it will operate needs further consideration. In particular, the issue of accountability needs to be addressed.

And devolved government requires a change in the mindset of central government: it has got to learn to 'let go'. ■

**Footnotes**

[1] Thanks are due to Colin Knox and Norman Gibson for comments on an earlier draft.
[2] *The Agreement: agreement reached in the multi-party negotiations*, Cm 3883, 1998
[3] David Heald, 'Formula-based territorial public expenditure in the United Kingdom', Aberdeen papers in accountancy, finance and management W7, University of Aberdeen, 1992
[4] Norman Gibson, 'Northern Ireland and Westminster: fiscal decentralisation—a public economics perspective', in Northern Ireland Economic Council, *Decentralised Government and Economic Performance in Northern Ireland*, Belfast, 1996
[5] C Thain and M Wright, *The Treasury and Whitehall: The Planning and Control of Public Expenditure, 1976-1993*, Clarendon, Oxford, 1995
[6] Heald, 'Territorial public expenditure in the UK', *Public Administration*, no 72, 1994, pp 147-75
[7] Thain and Wright, op cit, p324
[8] If expenditure on services in Britain equivalent to those in the Northern Ireland block decreased by £100, then the Northern Ireland block would be reduced by £2.87.
[9] In 1976-96, percentage population change was: Northern Ireland +9.1, England +5.2, Wales +4.4 and Scotland -2.0 (Office of National Statistics, *Population Trends*, spring 1998).
[10] Heald, Evidence to the Treasury Committee, *Second Report: The Barnett Formula*, House of Commons (HC 341), London, 1997. The switch from volume to cash planning may also determine the process of convergence. For instance, instead of baselines being indexed to inflation—thereby reducing its impact—they are raised (from year two of the survey to the new year three) by 2 per cent.
[11] When the Treasury Committee requested

comparative expenditures, the Treasury produced the following figures, stressing they represented broad orders of magnitude only: "In 1995/96, for Scottish block spending of around £13.7bn or £2670 per head, equivalent spending in England was around £98.7bn or £2020 per head; for Welsh block spending of some £6.5bn or £2230 per head, 'English equivalent' spending was some £87.2bn or £1780 per head; for Northern Ireland block spending of £7.7bn or £4680 per head, the 'English equivalent' was £173.3bn or £3540 per head." (Treasury Committee, March 1998, HC 619, p vii)

[12] Treasury Committee, 1997, Q77
[13] Heald, 1997, op cit
[14] Thain and Wright, op cit, p325
[15] Treasury Committee, 1998, op cit
[16] *Scotland's Parliament*, Cm 3658, §7.4
[17] Treasury, *Needs Assessment Study: Report*, HMSO, London, 1979
[18] Treasury Committee, 1997, op cit
[19] ibid, Q1
[20] K Bloomfield and C Carter, 'Introduction', in *People and Government: Questions for Northern Ireland*, Chief Executives' Forum/Joseph Rowntree Foundation, 1998, p5
[21] J M Mintz and T A Wilson, 'The allocation of tax authority: the Canadian federation', in R W Boadway, T J Courchene and D D Purvis eds, *Economic Dimensions of Constitutional Change*, John Deutsch Institute for the Study of Economic Policy, Queen's University, Ontario, 1991
[22] Cases can also be made for some power to modify the rate of corporation tax, for example, to stimulate investment. But it is doubtful whether this can be done within EU policy constraints and problems arise in the regional attribution of profits if companies operate in more than one jurisdiction.
[23] Treasury Committee, 1997, ibid
[24] 'Northern Ireland: towards a prosperous future', Northern Ireland Information Service release, May 12th 1998
[25] Similar problems arise in attempts to assess the impact of the public sector on personal distribution of income. The most significant tax expenditures include: occupational tax exemptions, mortgage-interest exemptions, corporation-tax capital allowances, capital-gains-tax exemptions and income-tax allowances. For the fiscal year 1997-98 tax expenditures are estimated to total some £95 billion.
[26] E Ahmad, 'Intergovernmental transfers: an international perspective', in Ahmad ed, *Financing Decentralised Expenditures*, Edward Elgar, Cheltenham, 1997
[27] J-L Migue, *Federalism and Free Trade*, Institute of Economic Affairs, London, 1993
[28] Deadweight effects in economics appear where an activity is subsidised which would have taken place even if the subsidy had not been granted.
[29] Barnett and Hutchinson, 'Public/private wage differentials in a regional economy: the case of Northern Ireland', *Ulster Papers in Public Policy and Management*, no 72, 1998
[30] There are a number of methodological problems associated with the public-expenditure/GDP ratio. One component, transfer payments, forms part of the numerator but not the denominator. A proportion of public expenditure will be consumed on imported goods and services which are not part of GDP. And public expenditure figures cover financial years, whereas GDP is calculated across calendar years.
[31] See J V Simpson, 'The finances of the public sector in Northern Ireland: 1968-1978', *Journal of the Statistical and Social Inquiry Society of Ireland*, vol XXIV, part II, 1980.
[32] Aside from the previous qualifications relating to the ratio, the decline in the PE/GDP ratio in Northern Ireland needs to be

interpreted with caution. First, the base year (1979-80) represents a period when public expenditure was particularly high and, secondly, the ratio is still 18 percentage points higher than the UK average in 1995-96.

[33] Analysis of the public expenditure/GDP ratio across 20 OECD countries, over the period 1960-1990, found a decline in several cases, particularly between 1985 and 1990. See P A McNutt, *The Economics of Public Choice*, Edward Elgar, Cheltenham, 1996.

[34] H Oxley and J P Martin, 'Controlling government spending and deficits: trends in the 1980s and prospects for the 1990s', *OECD Economic Studies* 17, 1991

[35] Simpson, op cit

[36] M Smyth, 'The public sector and the economy', in P Teague ed, *The Economy of Northern Ireland: Perspectives for Structural Change*, Lawrence and Wishart, London, 1993

[37] Department of Economic Development, Belfast, 1987 and 1990 respectively

[38] G Esping-Andersen, *The Three Worlds of Welfare Capitalism*, Polity, Cambridge, 1990

[39] Department of Finance and Personnel, *Northern Ireland Commentary on Public Expenditure Plans 1990-91 to 1992-93*, Belfast, 1990, p3

[40] See Thain and Wright, op cit, p490 and P M Jackson, 'Planning, control and the contract state', in D Corry ed, *Public Expenditure, Effective Management and Control,* Institute for Public Policy Research/Dryden Press, London, 1997, p229.

[41] Cm 3978, 1998

[42] op cit, p318

[43] Standing Advisory Commission on Human Rights, *Employment Equality: Building for the Future*, Cm 3684, Stationery Office, Belfast, 1997

[44] Cm 3890, 1998

[45] Department of Finance and Personnel, *Northern Ireland Expenditure Plans and Priorities: The Government's Expenditure Plans 1998-99 to 2000-01*, Stationery Office: London, 1998

[46] Thain and Wright, op cit

[47] B Black, 'Collective bargaining structure in Northern Ireland: dimensions, determinants and development', *Journal of the Statistical and Social Enquiry Society of Ireland*, vol XXV, part II, 1984-85

[48] NIO expenditure is negotiated and agreed separately with the Treasury—see Thain and Wright, op cit, p323

[49] Thain, 'Squaring the circle in public spending', *Parliamentary Brief*, vol 5, no 3, 1998, p24

[50] ibid

[51] 'Mo Mowlam welcomes £1.4 billion additional spending in Northern Ireland', Northern Ireland Information Service, July 14th 1998

[52] Treasury, *Stability and Investment for the Long Term: Economic and Fiscal Strategy Report*, Cm 3978, Stationery Office, London, 1998

[53] V N Hewitt, 'The public sector', in Harris, Jefferson and Spencer eds, *The Northern Ireland Economy: A Comparative Study in the Economic Development of a Peripheral Region*, Longman, London, 1990

[54] P McKeown, R Barnett and G Byrne, *An Initial Analysis of the Impact of Formula Funding and Local Management of Schools on the Management of Northern Ireland Schools: A School's Perspective*, Research Report Series, Department of Education Northern Ireland, Belfast, 1997

[55] Institute for Fiscal Studies, *The IFS Green Budget*, London, 1998

[56] Although one aspect of current policy might be dropped—that access should not be a key determinant in the review—there will be a public-expenditure cost to this.

[57] As we note above, public wages set UK-wide

may hinder the performance of the regional economy. From a social viewpoint, however, this might be viewed as an acceptable constraint on economic performance.

[58] Cm 3883, p5

[59] C Knox, 'Local government', in Bloomfield and Carter eds, op cit

[60] G Quigley, 'Opening remarks', in NIEC, op cit

[61] P Teague and J McCarthy, 'Big differences that matter: labour market systems in Ireland, north and south', in J Bradley ed, *The Two Economies of Ireland: Public Policy, Growth and Employment*, Oak Tree Press, Dublin, 1995

[62] Cm 3883, p17

[63] Teague and McCarthy, op cit

# Fiscal opportunities

**David Heald**[1]

Viewed from Scotland, where the constitutional-reform agenda was promoted by the broadly-based Scottish Constitutional Convention throughout the 90s,[2] the pace of developments in Northern Ireland has been spellbinding. Thus the month between the constitutional referendum and the election of the Northern Ireland Assembly should be compared with the corresponding 20-month gap in Scotland and Wales.

Yet it is essential to set political developments in Northern Ireland within the context of constitutional developments across the United Kingdom. Having elected devolved bodies in all three territories will be of enormous practical significance: for example, a Scottish Parliament on its own would have been much more vulnerable to interventions from Westminster and Whitehall.

Despite different forms of devolution in Scotland, Wales and Northern Ireland, the common feature of elected territorial bodies will alter the calculus of electoral competition: a UK party which alienated all three could only win a UK election on the back of a landslide majority in England. Consequently, a broad swathe of political opinion will seek to make the new institutions work, with the result that parties and voters in Great Britain will have to adapt to the direct and indirect consequences of proportional representation. The cumulative effect will be that the new constitutional arrangements will be able organically to mature, not necessarily frozen as they stand after the 1998 bout of constitutional legislation.

There are, however, interesting differences between the three territories. First, the run-up to devolution in Scotland is proving fraught: Scottish Office ministers are simultaneously condemned for lack of policy dynamism *and* for pre-empting

**David Heald sets the fiscal context straight**

the Parliament. The situation in Northern Ireland is quite different, not least because direct-rule ministers will not have careers in the Assembly.

Secondly, challenges to the devolution settlement can be expected to come from different directions. The Scottish referendum was decisive enough to end the system of administrative devolution, but the issue of devolution versus independence was not tested. The referendum in Wales dramatically highlighted its east-west divide, with vocal opponents decrying even non-legislative devolution as a step too far. In Northern Ireland, at the time of writing, it remains unclear whether those opposed to the establishment of the Assembly will seek to make it work.

Thirdly, there are some important differences in financial context. It seems likely that both Scotland and Northern Ireland have fared well out of the Barnett formula arrangements—their expenditure relatives probably having been kept at a higher level than their needs relatives. In comparison, Wales may have done less well.[3]

Fourthly, only the Scottish Parliament has an explicit tax-varying power (the 'tartan tax'[4]); the Northern Ireland Assembly has legislative powers without revenue-raising powers, while the Welsh Assembly has neither. There is a broad academic consensus that elected bodies should be fiscally responsible at the margin, especially when they have legislative powers.[5]

The key qualifier is 'at the margin': after the fiscal equalisation system has compensated for differences in needs and resources (that is, taxable capacity), the cost of additional expenditure (and the benefit of lower expenditure) should fall on 'local' taxpayers. There are powerful economic factors, including globalisation and membership of the European Union, which mean that sub-national governments cannot be fully self-financing.[6] There are encouraging signs that the decisiveness of the Scottish referendum result has persuaded some of those hitherto opposed to devolution to abandon 'tax-horror' stories and now support (more extensive) tax-varying powers.[7]

Fifthly, local authorities and their expenditure constitute a large claim on the Scottish and Welsh blocks, whereas their limited role in Northern Ireland means that a much larger proportion of its block will be under the direct control of the Assembly. Nevertheless, there remain important connections with the local-government finance system in Great Britain which will affect public expenditure in Northern Ireland (see below).

The Barnett formula has often been misrepresented and even more frequently misunderstood. Briefly, as described in the previous chapter, the formula has provided that changes in public expenditure in Scotland and in Wales for specific services within the territorial blocks would be determined according to the formula consequences of changes in comparable expenditure in England.[8]

Having previously been recalibrated in 1992, the formula proportions will now be updated annually, in line with revised estimates of relative populations, with effect from 1999-2000 (the first year to be affected by the results of the Comprehensive Spending Review). The revised ratio of comparable expenditure changes (based on mid-1996 population estimates) is England: Scotland: Wales = 100: 10.45: 5.95, with Northern Ireland adjusted to receive 2.91 per cent of the change in Great Britain.

Figure 1 demonstrates how the

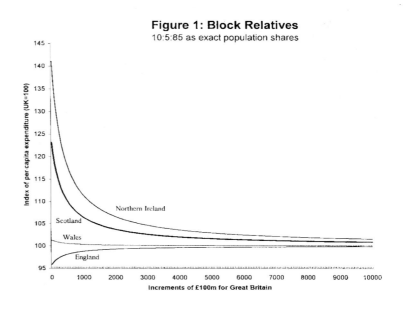

**Figure 1: Block Relatives**
10:5:85 as exact population shares

internal dynamic of this formula, when implemented over a period in which all increments of expenditure pass through the formula, will bring about convergence of *per capita* expenditure in all four territories.[9] But this conclusion depends on the assumptions that the initial formula proportions exactly match relative populations, that relative populations do not change through time and that there is no formula bypass.

Figure 2 modifies the assumption of exact matching, introducing instead the historical fact that the original formula proportions were advantageous to Scotland (10/85 rather than 9.57/85.31 as at mid-year 1976) and disadvantageous to Wales (5/85 rather than 5.12/85.31). Even though the Northern Ireland formula was expressed to two decimal places (2.75) in relation to its base of Great Britain, there was an adverse rounding as the population percentage at mid-year 1976 was 2.79.[10] As a result of the population rounding in the formula, Scotland's relative in Figure 2 does not fully converge, while Wales' overshoots and falls below 100.

Taken together, the 1992 recalibration (which moved the GB component of the formula to two decimal places) and the 1997 modification (annual population updating) have eliminated rounding as an inhibitor of long-run convergence. Nevertheless, there remains the issue of relative population change.

The contrast between Scotland and Northern Ireland is particularly marked. The population ratio of Scotland to England has changed from 11.24 per cent in 1976 to 10.45 per cent in 1996. In contrast, Northern Ireland's population ratio to Great Britain has risen from 2.79 to 2.91 per cent. Therefore, the convergence effect of application of the Barnett formula on *per capita* expenditure relatives has been attenuated in Scotland but accentuated in Northern Ireland.

Figure 3 illustrates for Northern Ireland the inevitable downside of a formula which does not challenge the base but allocates incremental expenditure on a population basis. Arithmetically, it must be the case that, starting from a higher *per capita* base, expenditure in Northern Ireland will rise more slowly (expressing, that is, each increment as a proportion of existing expenditure) than expenditure elsewhere in the United Kingdom.

At the beginning of the convergence process, started by the adoption of the Barnett formula in the context of then actual expenditure relatives, the increase in expenditure in Northern Ireland would be approximately 70 per cent of that in Great Britain. The growth relatives with England and Wales are little different from that with Great Britain. In contrast, the comparable initial figure for Northern Ireland with Scotland would be about 85 per cent—a result of Scotland's own convergence process. Naturally, the more expenditure has gone through the formula (the further right one goes along the horizontal axis), the closer these relatives tend to 100.

The Barnett formula has not, however, been operated on this 'clean' basis. First, there appears to have been considerable formula bypass: not all incremental expenditure has gone through the formula. Several examples have been instanced, confirmed by the Treasury in evidence to the Treasury Committee.[11] The extent of bypass has not been quantified, though it now occurs less frequently than in the 80s. Most of the identified cases seem to have benefited, rather than disadvantaged, the territories.[12]

Secondly, and much less publicly documented, the Treasury has on at least one occasion implemented an across-the-board percentage reduction in departmental baselines, before applying the formula. Whether by accident or design, this procedure allows ministers to state that the Barnett formula has been implemented, even though it erodes the protection afforded by the formula to inherited expenditure.[13]

Thirdly, the metropolitan domination

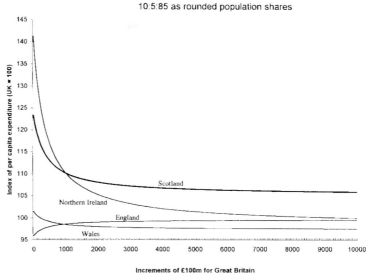

Figure 2: Block Relatives
10:5:85 as rounded population shares

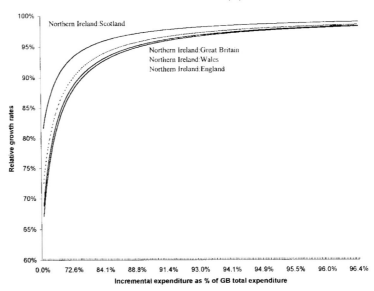

Figure 3: Relative Block Growth Rates
10:5:85 as rounded population shares

of UK politics should never be underestimated. The territorial fiscal system is of asymmetrical importance: it is crucial for the territorial departments and their ministers but often fairly invisible to their counterparts at the centre. Joel Barnett's memoirs of his experiences as chief secretary to the Treasury (1974-79)[14] never mention the eponymous formula—an omission to which his attention was drawn during the high-profile Treasury Committee hearing on November 13th 1997.[15] Similarly, Roy Jenkins' 22-page chapter on George Goschen, one of his predecessors as chancellor of the exchequer (1887-92), never mentions the Goschen formula; the present Scottish secretary, Donald Dewar, noted this omission in his book review.[16]

Nevertheless, while sometimes feeling slighted, the territorial departments have appreciated the advantages of their expenditure constituting a relatively small proportion of the UK total—not least because the Treasury's focus on the 'big numbers' keeps their programmes out of view most of the time. This is one reason why having a territorial formula has long been viewed as mutually beneficial.[17]

Devolution will markedly alter the context in which the formula is operated. First, the Barnett formula will become a mechanism for transferring money *between tiers of government*, not a mechanism *internal to one government*.[18] The intensity of political and media interest over the last 18 months gives some indication of what the future holds. The lack of transparency characterising the past use of the formula will be unsustainable. (The Treasury did not publish figures for expenditure comparable to the territorial blocks until March 1998, and even then the form of publication was singularly uninformative.[19])

Secondly, the effects of the formula can be modified by unconnected changes in the technical detail of public-expenditure management.[20] For example, the switch from volume to cash planning in 1982-83 increased the expenditure which would in principle pass through the formula. Previously, the territorial blocks had been revalued by specific price factors each year before the formula was applied to the growth component; subsequently, both the growth and inflation components would pass through the formula. Other things being equal, this would speed up convergence.

Thirdly, the financial arrangements for devolution are being devised at a time when there is substantial flux in UK public-expenditure planning. Until the new contours are more clearly visible, it is almost impossible to establish the detailed implications for the territorial expenditure system. One such change is resource accounting and budgeting in central government. This will bring both accruals accounting (in which capital assets are valued and depreciated) and resource budgeting, under which the planning system will be operated in accruals terms, and supply will be voted at a disaggregated level in accruals and at a more aggregated level in cash.[21] Formula consequences could in future be worked out in accruals, in cash or both.

Another change is that the Treasury has established a new fiscal framework as from 1999-2000, involving a three-year plan,[22] the replacement of the control total by two new aggregates (departmental expenditure limits and annually managed expenditure)[23] and the promulgation of fiscal rules as part of a statutory *Code for Fiscal Stability*. The necessary modifications to the territorial expenditure system have not yet been agreed between the Treasury and territorial departments, but experience suggests not all the implications will be fully anticipated.

Despite attracting little attention at the UK level, the pre-devolution system of territorial government embodied extensive devolution of expenditure responsibilities.[24] The essence of contemporary constitutional reforms is to transfer these responsibilities from members of the UK cabinet to those who owe their position and legitimacy to the elected territorial assemblies. The issue of 'local' fiscal accountability has naturally acquired more salience.[25] The devolved bodies should eventually have more responsibility for raising revenue at the margin.

This judgment should not be taken as encouragement to the Northern Ireland Assembly to think in terms of spending more. *Per capita* expenditure in Northern Ireland exceeds the UK average by a large margin.[26] Revenue-raising should be regarded as a means of securing fiscal accountability at the margin, and of securing proper attention to the full range of allocative and distributional effects of public-expenditure programmes. Given the likelihood of downwards pressure on the expenditure relative in the medium term, greater awareness is needed in Northern Ireland of the relevant opportunity costs of public-sector activity.

Some financing issues are highly technical but others have constitutional and political importance. It is useful to distinguish them at three levels: the United Kingdom as a whole, most notably in the financing of local government; those arising as a consequence of devolution in the three territories; and those specific to Northern Ireland.

Fiscal accountability at the margin can only be secured for the devolved bodies following a thorough review of sub-national taxation. Indeed, the financing of devolved assemblies is intricately interwoven with questions about the financing of local authorities.[27] This is more obvious in Great Britain than in Northern Ireland, where local authorities are less important spenders because of their much narrower functional responsibilities. Northern Ireland is nevertheless affected by these interconnections through the operation of the Barnett formula.

For reasons which were entirely predictable and understandable, the pre-referendum debate in Scotland about financial aspects of devolution concentrated heavily upon the 'tartan tax' and its possible repercussions on the formula. Even the 1998 Scotland Bill contains little about many important financial issues, preferring to leave them to be tackled administratively or by legislation by the new Parliament. The priority of the devolved bodies should be to review systematically the value for money secured from existing programmes. Nevertheless, the Scottish Parliament needs to use the tax-varying power in the medium term, as it will otherwise atrophy.

The budgetary procedures of the devolved bodies should take account of those taxes and charges which, because of netting off, reduce the amount of expenditure scored against the block. Naturally, this highlights the importance of establishing a good working relationship with local government. In Scotland, the term 'concordat' has been used; the Commission on Local Government and the Scottish Parliament has been tasked to report to the Scottish first minister when that person is elected.

There was a warning in the Scottish devolution white paper that 'excessive growth' in local-authority self-financed expenditure, relative to England, might be scored against the assigned budget—though there was no guidance on what 'excessive' might be: "Should self-financed expenditure start to rise steeply, the Scottish Parliament would clearly come under pressure from council-tax payers in Scotland to exercise the capping powers. If growth relative to England were excessive and were such as to threaten targets set for public expenditure as part of the management of the UK economy, and the Scottish Parliament nevertheless chose not to exercise its powers, it would be open to the UK government to take the excess into account in considering the level of their support for expenditure in Scotland."[28] This seems likely to be an area of delicate negotiation between the UK government and the devolved executives. There would only be scope for a sustained switch of the burden of financing a given level of sub-national expenditure if there were a UK-wide consensus about the desirability of such a change.[29]

Moreover, UK-wide rules are urgently required on a series of technical issues which have considerable potential for generating political conflict. Obvious examples relate to the treatment of European Union funds, National Lottery grants, assets financed through the Private Finance Initiative and tax expenditures granted by the UK government which touch upon devolved programme areas. Each opens up scope for budgetary gamesmanship and poor value for money, suggesting regulation by the Territorial Exchequer Board proposed below.

Whereas finance was rightly seen as crucial to debates about Scottish devolution, the main issue in Northern Ireland was a lasting peace settlement. The inevitable consequence is that several issues have not received a public airing.

There has been considerable media discussion of the distributional effects of peace in Northern Ireland. In the long run, there would be downwards pressure on the real incomes of middle-class households (especially those currently benefiting from GB-pegged wages and low house prices), although in the short run this would be masked by windfall capital gains as house prices rose in response to stronger GDP growth.

Given the macro-economic importance attached to house-price inflation by Muellbauer[30]—who believes that residential property is too lightly taxed under the council-tax system in Great Britain—the Assembly should consider carefully the desirable path of regional and district rates. As a result of the Comprehensive Spending Review, there has been an important change in the public-expenditure treatment of the regional rate.[31] Whereas hitherto it has only been a financing matter—in the sense that its level did not affect expenditure totals—variations upwards or downwards will in future directly affect how much can be spent.

Unquestionably, there will be difficulties ahead as public expenditure will be tight and considerable adjustment will be needed. The publicity attached to these difficulties, however, should not obscure the opportunities.

Starting with the difficulties, greater transparency of territorial fiscal arrangements is inevitable. The most likely outcome is some compression of expenditure relatives, particularly from levels which seem higher than (likely) needs relatives. This convergence needs to be accomplished in a gradual, non-disruptive way.

The possibility of this being achievable has been greatly enhanced by the favouring through the Comprehensive Spending Review of those functional areas which will be devolved.[32] For example, the substantial boosts to education and health expenditure in Great Britain have generated formula consequences for Northern Ireland.

Nevertheless, the 'managed block' (see below) will be unable to cope with the up-front costs of the retrenchment of 'law and order' expenditure; there will have to be non-formula supplements for this purpose. These will undoubtedly raise the question as to whether a proportion of subsequent savings on 'law and order' should be returned to the Treasury, rather than transferred to other programmes.

The Assembly should embrace transparency (as indeed should its counterparts in Scotland and Wales). It will provide the best long-run protection of its autonomy and educate the public. This naturally entails risks, though these already exist.[33] The finance ministries of the devolved executives should commence advance planning for a UK-wide needs assessment in the medium term.

The ineffectiveness of the Northern Ireland Joint Exchequer Board,[34] though a warning of the dangers to be avoided, should not discourage the establishment of a Territorial Exchequer Board on the Australian model.[35] Despite the obvious temptation in Scotland and Northern Ireland to postpone any discussion of expenditure relatives, it will be safer for the territories to see such machinery in place while the constitutional-reform agenda still enjoys a fair wind at Westminster.[36]

Turning to the opportunities, a key issue in Northern Ireland will be better value for money from block expenditure. Notwithstanding the problems of comparing expenditure levels, there can be no doubt, as remarked above, that *per capita* expenditure is well above the UK average. An observer would speculate that sustained peace should help improve value for money, as the security problem must have complicated public-service delivery across the board.

An urgent priority must be a review of the entire machinery of government, the complexity of which—for example, the education and library boards and the health and social services boards—suggests a use of quangos to legitimise direct rule. Once devolved government has been restored, there would seem to be potential savings from delayering.

This will not be painless: relatively well-paid jobs will disappear, with substantial, up-front redundancy costs. Moreover, the deflationary macroeconomic impact of a reduction in security-related expenditure—including that within the defence budget rather than the Northern Ireland programme—needs to be offset by strong private-sector performance. Clearly, much depends on the performance of the UK and Republic of Ireland economies during this transition.

Secondly, there is an excellent opportunity for constructing a more open budget process, in which well-researched information is available about programme performance and expenditure options. It should be possible to avoid the excesses of executive domination and news management which have characterised the UK Public Expenditure Survey in recent years.

For example, the Department of Finance & Personnel (DFP) should be obliged to provide costed options to Assembly committees. In the case of Scotland, the budgetary timetable has to be consistent with the practicalities of the Inland Revenue implementing the 'tartan tax' on a cost-effective basis. Across the United Kingdom, local authorities and a wide range of other public bodies need to be able to take their own budgetary decisions in the light of information about grant levels.

The principles governing the UK territorial fiscal system can be made accessible, notwithstanding the technical complexity of its detailed operation. The prevailing opacity has owed much to obsessive secrecy and limited institutional memory.

Thirdly, in comparison with Scotland and Wales, Northern Ireland possesses some advantages and some disadvantages—both rooted in its institutional and financial history. On the positive side, it already has much of the necessary financial framework and institutional infrastructure—for example, a separate estimates system and the Northern Ireland Audit Office, headed by the Comptroller and Auditor General for Northern Ireland. On the negative side, the frozen inheritance of provisions contained in, or originating from, the Government of Ireland Act 1920 has created something of a time warp.

In particular, a gulf has developed between the formal financial system and the reality of expenditure planning (which has increasingly become like that in Scotland and Wales). This effect has been reinforced by the suspension of 'normal' politics: for almost 25 years decisions have been taken by direct-rule ministers with no 'local' accountability, rendering the financial system opaque and little discussed. One indication is that the Northern Ireland Affairs Committee's recent inquiry into Northern Ireland programmes explored ground that Scotland had begun to traverse in 1980.[37]

One reason for such a lack of transparency may have been the sensitivity attached to Northern Ireland's relationship with the Republic. Repealing outdated provisions in the Government of Ireland Act 1920 could have raised unwelcome diplomatic and domestic complications.[38] The co-existence of statutorily required documents (reflecting continuing provisions from the period of devolved government) and Treasury-mandated documents (reflecting Northern Ireland's position within the UK public-expenditure system) has rendered the financial system inaccessible.

For example, it is difficult to see the relationship between the annually published *Public Income and Expenditure* (DFP), the *Finance Accounts of Northern Ireland* (ditto), the *Northern Ireland Appropriation Accounts* (Northern Ireland Audit Office) and the *Northern Ireland Departmental Report* (DFP & Treasury). The departmental report, which covers the Northern Ireland Office and Departments, is considerably less helpful than its Scottish and Welsh counterparts in explaining the territorial expenditure system.

Most notably, there is serious terminological confusion. What is described in the published documents as the 'Northern Ireland block' is not comparable to the Scottish and Welsh blocks. The best way to explain the structure of the Northern Ireland programme is to think in terms of three levels.

The first is the Northern Ireland programme, which corresponds to expenditure within the responsibility of the secretary of state; this is the focus of the departmental report. The second excludes expenditure on 'national' agricultural and fisheries support (these being greatly influenced by UK and EU policies); this is what is described in the departmental report as the 'Northern Ireland block'. The third level is described internally as the 'managed block', though there is no explicit reference to it in the 1997 or 1998 departmental reports; this is the aggregate corresponding to the Scottish and Welsh blocks, fed by the Barnett formula, and over which the secretary of state holds expenditure-switching discretion.[39]

The managed block thus includes expenditure by the Northern Ireland Office—predominantly on 'law and order'—as well as by Northern Ireland departments. The favourable security situation at the time of the 1994 Survey allowed the previous secretary of state to switch expenditure from 'law and order' into other programmes; the reverse occurred in 1996. There remain substantial uncertainties about how the system will operate under devolution: 'law and order' expenditure is 'reserved', remaining the responsibility of the secretary of state.

There should therefore be a thorough rationalisation of Northern Ireland public-finance documentation, including the preparation of a comprehensive overview along the lines already established for Scotland and Wales.[40]

A major educational exercise is also required, to improve the understanding of Assembly members and public servants of how the territorial fiscal system operates. Moreover, each of the major political groups in the Assembly should designate someone to develop the specialist expertise needed to engage in technical discussions with the financial managers of the Northern Ireland programme, most notably in the DFP. Senior civil servants involved in finance are likely to acquire much higher public exposure than during direct rule.

There is so much political capital tied up in making a success of the Assembly that the opportunities should outweigh the difficulties. And the developing UK context should reinforce the sense that much can be achieved.

MacKay and Audas admirably capture the need for decentralisation in their discussion of Wales: "Where government is has economic as well as political effects. In a centralised State, career structures develop which require location in or close to the national capital. That capital draws strength from the atmosphere of centralised culture and power. In the UK, there are few fields of endeavour where it is possible to scale the commanding heights without being close to the national capital."[41]

It will be interesting to observe how the United Kingdom as a whole adjusts to asymmetrical government.[42] The greatest irony is that this has long existed—but few outside the territories ever noticed. ■

## Footnotes

[1] This paper draws upon work financed by a sabbatical project on the financing of decentralised government funded by the Nuffield Foundation.

[2] Scottish Constitutional Convention, *Towards Scotland's Parliament* and *Scotland's Parliament, Scotland's Right*, Edinburgh, 1990 and 1995

[3] See D Richards, 'Oral evidence', in Treasury Committee, *The Barnett Formula*, Second Report of Session 1997-98, HC 341, Stationery Office, London, 1997. Firm conclusions can not be reached without a replication of the Treasury's 1979 expenditure needs assessment, which was embarked upon in the context of the then Labour government's devolution plans for Scotland and Wales (Treasury, *Needs Assessment Study—Report*, London, 1979). The 1997 devolution white papers for Scotland and Wales said there would not be fundamental change to the Barnett formula without a new needs assessment (Scottish Office, *Scotland's Parliament*, Cm 3658, Stationery Office, Edinburgh, 1997; Welsh Office, *A Voice for Wales: The*

*Government's Proposals for a Welsh Assembly*, Cm 3718, Stationery Office, London, 1997). In my view, Lord Barnett overstated the importance of relative GDP when he gave oral evidence to the Treasury Committee on November 13th 1997: given the services financed by the blocks, demographic structure and participation rates in publicly provided health and education will be more important determinants of relative need than relative GDP.

[4] D A Heald and N Geaughan, 'The tartan tax: devolved variation in income tax rates', *British Tax Review*, no 5, 1997, pp 337-48

[5] See D King, *Fiscal Tiers: The Economics of Multi-Level Government*, Allen and Unwin, London, 1984; D Bell, S Dow, King and N Massie, *Financing Devolution*, Hume Papers on Public Policy, vol 4, no 2, Edinburgh University Press, Edinburgh, 1996; L Blow, J Hall and S Smith, *Financing Regional Government in Britain*, Institute for Fiscal Studies, London, 1996; Constitution Unit, *Scotland's Parliament: Fundamentals for a New Scotland Act*, London, 1996; Heald and Geaughan, 'Financing a Scottish Parliament', in S Tindale ed, *The State and the Nations: The Politics of Devolution*, Institute for Public Policy Research, London, 1996; and S Smith, 'Regional government, fiscal and financial management in Northern Ireland', in Northern Ireland Economic Council, *Decentralised Government and Economic Performance in Northern Ireland*, Belfast, 1996.

[6] Heald, Geaughan and C Robb, 'Financial arrangements for UK devolution', *Regional & Federal Studies*, vol 8, no 1, 1998

[7] Many observers believe the imposition of the two-question Scottish referendum (first on devolution, separately on tax-varying powers) was designed to ditch the 'tartan tax'. Ironically, the result was the opposite. Allan Massie wrote in the *Scotsman* ('Common culture, but divided loyalties', August 24th 1998): "It may seem odd that those of us who argued against devolution should now wish the Scottish parliament to have more powers than it is to be granted. It is odd, but it is not illogical ... we can't believe that creating a parliament with the power to spend but without the responsibility of imposing taxes can either make for good government or prevent recurrent and damaging friction between London and Edinburgh."

[8] See the chapter by R Barnett and G Hutchinson in this volume.

[9] The intuition is quite straightforward. Over time, base expenditure (on which the three territories have *per capita* relatives above UK=100) becomes a smaller proportion of total block expenditure, with incremental expenditure (which has passed through the population-based formula) becoming a larger proportion.

[10] The combined effect is quite complicated. If the expenditure blocks were exactly coterminous and all expenditure went through the formula, the effect of rounding was that Scotland would obtain 9.73 per cent rather than 9.31 per cent of incremental UK expenditure (4.53 per cent higher); Wales would obtain 4.87 per cent rather than 4.98 per cent (2.31 per cent lower); England would obtain 82.73 per cent rather than 82.99 per cent (0.32 per cent lower); and Northern Ireland would obtain 2.68 per cent rather than 2.71 per cent (1.40 per cent lower).

[11] Heald, 'Territorial public expenditure in the United Kingdom', *Public Administration*, vol 72, Summer 1994; 'Memorandum submitted by HM Treasury' and 'Supplementary memorandum submitted by HM Treasury on Tuesday 16 December 1997', in Treasury Committee, op cit

[12] When, as on health, the territorial expenditure relative is substantially above that for the

United Kingdom as a whole, this is likely to reflect in part higher *per capita* employment of nurses. If the Treasury were to underwrite the full cost to each health department of a UK nurses' pay settlement, the territories would receive more than if the total UK cost of the award were to be distributed through the Barnett formula.

[13] Money 'saved' by applying a constant percentage cut to the territorial blocks and to comparable expenditure can then be passed through the Barnett formula, generating 'formula consequences' supplementary to those generated by year-on-year increases in comparable expenditure. Naturally, the arithmetical effect is disadvantageous to the territories because the constant percentage cut generates more 'savings' from their blocks than they subsequently receive back in these 'artificial' formula consequences.

[14] J Barnett, *Inside the Treasury*, André Deutsch, London, 1982

[15] G Radice, 'Oral evidence', in Treasury Committee, Q1, op cit

[16] R Jenkins, *The Chancellors*, Macmillan, London, 1998; D Dewar, 'Lives at No 11', *Scotland on Sunday*, August 23rd 1998

[17] The Goschen formula is even more badly documented than Barnett. It was enunciated in 1888 as a means of regulating changes in education expenditure, and continued to be used in some form until the late 1950s. The basis of the Goschen proportions was the assignment of probate duties in the rounded percentages of overall contributions to the exchequer. The Barnett formula has been used since 1978. The use for Scotland of one or other of these two formulae for approximately 90 of the last 110 years is indicative of the enduring appeal of such a mechanism. Formula links to public expenditure in Great Britain acquired importance in the financing of the Northern Ireland Parliament once the financial scheme of the Government of Ireland Act 1920 had effectively collapsed. The Colwyn formula, devised by the Northern Ireland Special Arbitration Committee in 1925, has been described by Norman Gibson ('Northern Ireland and Westminster: fiscal decentralisation—a public economics perspective', in NIEC op cit, p33) as "a kind of forerunner of the Barnett formula of some fifty years later". Moreover, it can also be seen as a successor to the Goschen formula, which had continued to operate in Great Britain. Significantly, Gibson observes that "none of this material was available for public scrutiny".

[18] Heald and Geaughan, 'Fiscal implications', in P Norton ed, *The Consequences of Devolution*, Hansard Society, London, 1998

[19] See 'Barnett formula: impact on relative public spending per head in England, Scotland, Wales and Northern Ireland', in Treasury Committee, *The Barnett Formula: The Government's Response to the Committee's Second Report of Session 1997-98*, Fourth Special Report of Session 1997-98, HC 619, appendix 2, Stationery Office, London, 1998. Expressed in terms of England=100 for that expenditure which is comparable with each territorial block—the coverages of which differ significantly—the block relatives for 1995-96 implied by the data are: Scotland 132, Wales 125 and Northern Ireland 132. In particular, the Northern Ireland figure is significantly affected by social-security expenditure being included in the comparison. While the Scotland relative is in line with the data for earlier years (see Heald, 1994, op cit), the Wales relative is considerably higher than would have been expected. Greater disaggregation is obviously required.

[20] See Heald, 1994, op cit. This can happen even when changes in the public-expenditure planning system have no immediate connection with policy on territorial programmes.

Some changes are not even announced by the Treasury. One of the sources of formula bypass identified in Heald, 1994, was the Treasury's practice of creating a baseline for the third year of each Survey by incorporating an automatic inflation adjustment. Not until December 1997 did it reach the public domain ('Supplementary memorandum ...', in Treasury Committee, 1997, op cit) that this practice had changed: "In Surveys since 1993 it has been the practice to create the year three baseline by rolling forward Year 2 cash plans at the same level in cash terms."

[21] Treasury, 'Resource accounting and budgeting', in Treasury Committee, *The New Fiscal Framework and the Comprehensive Spending Review*, vol II: minutes of evidence and appendices, Eighth Report of Session 1997-98, HC 960-II, Stationery Office, London, 1998. Strictly, for 'cash' should be read 'total financing requirement' (which extends beyond cash to include non-cash items such as local-authority credit approvals and capitalised Private Finance Initiative projects).

[22] The new expenditure planning system does not entail three-year rolling programmes; at present, there is a three-year horizon for departmental expenditure limits (1999-2000, 2000-01 and 2001-02) but the time horizon will successively shorten as these years arrive. Exceptionally, in 2000, a new set of three-year plans will be promulgated for 2001-02 to 2003-04, as a consequence of the introduction of resource budgeting.

[23] Treasury, *Stability and Investment for the Long Term: Economic and Fiscal Strategy Report 1998*, Cm 3978, Stationery Office, London, 1998

[24] Heald, *Financing Devolution within the United Kingdom: A Study of the Lessons from Failure*, Centre for Research on Federal Financial Relations, Australian National University Press, Canberra, 1980

[25] Heald, *Financing a Scottish Parliament: Options for Debate*, Scottish Foundation for Economic Research, Glasgow, 1990

[26] See Barnett and Hutchinson in this volume and Treasury, *Public Expenditure: Statistical Analyses 1998-99*, Cm 3901, Stationery Office, London, 1998.

[27] It is now widely argued that the market-extending reforms of the Thatcher and Major Conservative governments centralised power in the public sector, drastically limiting the effective discretion of local authorities in Great Britain. See A Gamble, *The Free Economy and the Strong State: The Politics of Thatcherism*, Macmillan, Basingstoke, 1994, and S Jenkins, *Accountable to None: The Tory Nationalization of Britain*, Hamish Hamilton, London, 1995.

[28] Scottish Office, *Scotland's Parliament*, op cit, 1997, §7.24

[29] There are complex interactions between local-government revenue raising and central-government expenditure; for example, part of incremental council-tax revenue will be met from the social-security budget. Moreover, local authorities have recognised that increasing council rents provides them with access to the social-security budget.

[30] J Muellbauer, 'X-rating the housing boom: reforming the council tax could do great things for the economy as a whole', *Observer*, May 4th 1997

[31] Department of Finance & Personnel and Treasury, *Northern Ireland Expenditure Plans and Priorities: The Government's Expenditure Plans 1997-98 to 1999-2000*, Cm 3616, Stationery Office, London, 1997; *Northern Ireland Expenditure Plans and Priorities: The Government's Expenditure Plans 1998-99*, Cm 3916, Stationery Office, London, 1998

[32] Treasury, *Modern Public Services for Britain: Investing in Reform—Comprehensive Spending Review: New Public Spending Plans*

*1999-2002*, Cm 4011, Stationery Office, London, 1998

[33] Anyone doubting this point is encouraged to watch the video of the Treasury Committee's November 13th 1997 evidence session on the Barnett formula.

[34] Gibson, op cit

[35] Heald and Geaughan, 1996, op cit

[36] Assessments of relative need are partly technical exercises and partly matters of political judgment—notably about what constitutes a policy, what is a consequence of policy discretion and what is a binding constraint. A Scottish example with obvious Northern Ireland resonance illustrates this point. Since 1918, there have been separate non-denominational and Catholic school systems, both managed by local authorities. This duplication undoubtedly imposes extra costs, particularly in the Scottish context of falling rolls. Treasury officials whose ministers were hostile to devolution might argue that these extra costs should be met entirely from Scottish resources. Needless to say, this would raise hugely sensitive issues because of the history of this separate provision. The purpose of a needs assessment would be to validate the continuing use of a Barnett-type formula; it would be contrary to the spirit of devolution to establish an annual mechanism like the revenue support grant for local authorities.

[37] Northern Ireland Affairs Committee, *Northern Ireland Public Expenditure: Current Plans and Priorities*, First Report of Session 1997-98, HC 295, and *Response by the Government to the First Report from the Northern Ireland Affairs Committee, Session 1997-98: Northern Ireland Public Expenditure: Current Plans and Priorities*, First Special Report of Session 1997-98, HC 700—both Stationery Office, London, 1998; Committee on Scottish Affairs, *Scottish Aspects of the 1980-84 Public Expenditure White Paper: Minutes of Evidence, Monday 7 July 1980, together with Appendices*, HC 689 of Session 1979-80, HMSO, London, 1980

[38] Gibson, op cit

[39] Two further points should be noted. First, the Northern Ireland programme is narrower than identifiable expenditure in Northern Ireland, as annually published by the Treasury, but much less so than for Scotland and Wales (largely because it includes social-security benefit expenditure). Secondly, there is public expenditure which takes place in Northern Ireland but which falls within the category the Treasury treats as non-identified (most obviously, the costs of the army presence).

[40] Scottish Office, *Government Expenditure and Revenue in Scotland, 1995-96*, Glasgow, 1997; Welsh Office, *Government Expenditure and Revenue—Wales, 1994-95*, Cardiff, 1997

[41] R R MacKay and R P Audas, 'The economic impact of a Welsh Assembly', in MacKay, Audas, G Holtham and B Morgan, *The Economic Impact of a Welsh Assembly*, Institute of Welsh Affairs, Cardiff, 1997, p23

[42] M Keating, 'What's wrong with asymmetrical government?', in H Elcock and Keating eds, *Remaking the Union: Devolution and British Politics in the 1990s* (special issue of *Regional & Federal Studies*, vol 8, no 1), Frank Cass, London, 1998

# Conclusion

**Paul Gorecki**[1]

The governance of the United Kingdom is entering uncharted waters, with the creation of devolved institutions in Wales, Scotland and Northern Ireland. No longer will public-expenditure levels and priorities be set in London by a single government consisting of one party responsible for the whole of the UK, with some adaptation to suit regional needs and circumstances.

Instead, regionally elected and accountable politicians will have a much greater voice in determining these levels and priorities in their respective jurisdictions. While there will be differences reflecting the particular powers and responsibilities devolved across Wales, Scotland and Northern Ireland, there will also be common concerns that transcend these differences.

Several important themes emerged from the round-table. Although its focus was firmly on Northern Ireland, there will be resonances in Wales and Scotland. Indeed, there should be ample opportunity for each jurisdiction to learn from the others as the devolution process gathers steam.

Four themes are worth developing:
• Is the Barnett formula for determining public expenditure sustainable?
• Should the new Assembly have taxation powers?
• Are Northern Ireland's attitudes to public expenditure tenable?
• Can and will public-expenditure priorities differ radically under the Assembly?

It was argued by several of the contributors to the seminar that the Barnett formula had worked to Northern Ireland's advantage since introduced in 1979. Public expenditure *per capita* had started off well above that in Great Britain when the formula was first applied. And while strict application should have led to gradual convergence with the rest of the UK, this had not happened to the extent anticipated. Decisions on public expenditure had been made outside the formula and these had benefited the disadvantaged territories, including Northern Ireland.

There can be no automatic assumption, however, that the Barnett formula will survive the devolutionary process as the basis for allocating public expenditure across the UK. Although it was designed at a time when devolution was being considered, it has never actually been tested in that environment. Instead of being a method for allocating public expenditure between different tiers of government, Barnett has been a convenient mechanism—often misrepresented and even more frequently misunderstood, according to David Heald—for transferring money internally within one government. There can be no guarantee it will survive in the new context.

Indeed Barnett is already the subject of much debate in England. The initial stages of the London mayoral election led to headlines such as 'London "subsidises rest of UK by up to £14bn"'.[2] The North East Chamber of Commerce, Trade and Industry argues that much has changed since Barnett was introduced and these changes need to be reflected in a revised formula—otherwise, inequality of treatment will continue. If this rising chorus of disapproval continues—as seems likely as regional development agencies and chambers are created in England—the issue of territorial public-expenditure allocation is unlikely to go away.

Thus the perceived favourability of Northern Ireland's public-expenditure treatment is likely to be increasingly questioned. Sooner or later, a new method of allocating territorial expenditure across the UK will be devised, to ensure broad democratic support is sustained. In countries like Canada, which have a federal structure and explicit rules for allocating expenditure between levels of government, changes of circumstance—such as the OPEC oil-price hikes of the 70s or the federal government's large debt in the 80s—cause the rules to be re-examined. Recently, the European Commission has raised the whole issue of how EU contributions are distributed across the various member states. As circumstances change so policy needs to be reassessed.

It is frequently argued—and with good reason—that governments should be accountable to the electorate in raising taxes to pay for the public services provided by the state. There are costs associated with higher taxes: loss of efficiency, administrative expenditure and reductions in personal or corporate income. These need to be offset against the benefits of public expenditure, such as provision of health care, education, social security and reduced inequality.

If the costs and benefits are considered at the same time, the size of the state should expand to the point where the marginal or additional benefit provided by a public service is equated to the marginal or extra cost represented by a tax. Different political parties offer different packages to the electorate, as they seek to find the trade-off preferred by sufficient voters to win an election.

Since Northern Ireland is part of a centralised rather than decentralised or federal state, such a procedure does not occur. Levels of taxation and public expenditure are determined separately. Furthermore, given the substantial difference between tax revenues and public expenditure—a deficit of the order of several billion pounds—the level of taxation required to pay for regional public services in full would be prohibitive. Smith, for example, estimates that the standard rate of income tax would have to increase from 24 to 55 per cent, and the top rate from 40 to 91 per cent, if all Northern Ireland public expenditure were to be financed by regional taxation.[3]

It is not uncommon in multi-tier government systems, however, for a level in receipt of substantial net contributions from a higher tier to be given some tax-varying powers at the margin. In other words, instead of full accountability (all public expenditure at that level funded through taxation at that level), there is marginal accountability (tax voted at that level covering only a portion of expenditure at that level).

Scotland's Parliament, for example, will have the power to vary the standard rate of income tax by 3p in the pound. Such a power has the advantage that should the devolved legislature wish to spend more than is set by the higher level of government, the lower tier has the ability to do so. It can help avoid unproductive disagreements between different levels of government.

There are no proposals in the Belfast agreement for the Assembly to have tax-varying powers. While the existing power over the regional property rate will remain, Smith shows convincingly this is not a good base for regional taxation.[4] By far the best is a regional income tax. Thus Northern Ireland—for reasons of accountability and efficiency—should eventually adopt a regional taxation system, based on income rather than property.

Attitudes to the role of the public sector have changed dramatically in the world since World War II. As John Loughlin indicated, there has been a movement away from the 'expanding welfare' state of the late 40s and 50s, through the 'contracting neo-liberal' model of the 80s and 90s, to an 'enabling communitarian/social' variant in the late 90s—this last could be described as 'neo-liberalism with a human face'. Northern Ireland operates in this wider framework, which shows, as Vani Borooah notes, every sign of being less than receptive to substantial increases in public expenditure in relation to gross domestic product.

Public expenditure is large in relation to the regional economy: its ratio to GDP is around 60 per cent, compared with 40 per cent for the UK as a whole. Furthermore, there seems to be a pervasive view in Northern Ireland that public expenditure, or some other aspect of public policy, always holds the key to resolving a particular problem.

At its worst, this results in a 'dependency culture' that permeates all sectors of the economy and inefficient public-policy decisions (because regional policy failures are funded by central government); at its best it brings imaginative and innovative policy interventions. Yet no matter whether one favours a malign or benign perspective on this, what is striking is that the implicit model harks back to the expansive welfare state of the immediate aftermath of the second world war. Things have moved on.

This dissonance may in some measure reflect the lack of any relationship between tax and public expenditure in Northern Ireland, the substantial growth in the public sector in the 70s—when the state successfully alleviated such important social problems as bad housing—and a quarter century in which regional politicians were in permanent opposition. Irrespective of the reason, however, some adjustment will be required in the degree to which the state can be expected to solve the economic and social problems of Northern Ireland.

The establishment of devolved institutions creates the opportunity for regional preferences to determine where public expenditure should be allocated, what services should be provided and the delivery mechanism(s) through which this should take place. Much public expenditure in the regional economy relates to 'transferred' matters and thus comes within the ambit of these new institutions, particularly the Assembly.

This, theoretically at least, raises the possibility that priorities and the resulting pattern of public expenditure could be radically altered. Yet, while there will clearly be greater differences between Great Britain and Northern Ireland, it would seem much more likely that any changes—initially at least—will be gradual and at the margin.

Radical change in the role of the state and the pattern of public expenditure typically takes place with strong governments which have a sense of direction. The Labour government of 1945 ushered in the welfare state, while the Conservative governments of the 80s set the new-right agenda. In both cases, the change in government was the signal for the advent of a new model of the role of the state, a decisive break with the past—a break accepted, albeit with some modification, by successive governments of a different political complexion.

In the devolved institutions of Northern Ireland, no one party has overall control. Indeed, government is by an involuntary coalition which spans parties with quite different ideologies and support bases. Furthermore, it is not clear where the locus of power will reside: the Executive Committee? the minister? the relevant Assembly committee? This suggests that compromise and marginal change will be the hallmark of governance. Indeed, as a leading political scientist in Northern Ireland recently observed, the first and deputy first minister have a vision of moving Northern Ireland politics towards "a middle ground consensus".[5]

In addition, although Northern Ireland will have devolved institutions, it will still be operating within the UK system of governance. To the extent that the policies and priorities of the UK seem attractive to voters in Northern Ireland, there will a tendency to follow that lead. Recall that in the 40s the then Stormont government was reluctant to introduce some of Labour's welfare-state reforms, but the pressure was eventually irresistible.

The strong ties across the UK, in terms of pay and conditions, arising from UK-wide collective bargaining are likely to limit the possibility of a social-partnership model, such as that practised in the Republic of Ireland. Nevertheless, the continued economic success of the republic will likely result in an assessment of how binding such constraints are in applying its social-partnership model to Northern Ireland. The region will still receive considerable fiscal transfers from the rest of the UK, which will mean the Treasury will continue to exert pressure and influence.

Finally, if Northern Ireland were to follow policies that differed radically from those of the rest of the UK, and if these were to fail, then the issue would arise as to who, if anybody, would bail the region out. Given the tight constraints on public expenditure and the above discussion, it would appear the answer would be Northern Ireland voters—in terms of lower expenditure on health and education. Risk-averse politicians are unlikely to follow policies that could result in such an outcome.

Despite considerable theoretical discretion over spending, therefore, it seems likely rapid change will not occur. But politicians need to walk before they can run—to learn the ropes of administration and democratic accountability—particularly when the structures are so novel. Thus while change at first might be marginal, as time elapses and politicians learn their roles better, bolder decisions will increasingly be the order of the day.

Northern Ireland, according to several contributors to the round-table, has done relatively well in public-expenditure terms since 1979. But the changed circumstances of devolution will mean that the current method of allocation across the UK will be reassessed and Northern Ireland is likely to receive less public expenditure than would otherwise be the case. Increased public accountability suggests that the Assembly should have limited powers over regional income taxation, as proposed for Scotland. This would, of course, be in addition to—not a replacement for—the level of public expenditure set by Barnett or any successor. Although the Assembly has theoretically wide discretion over priorities, powerful forces will operate, in the short term at least, to preserve the *status quo*.

Thus public expenditure in Northern Ireland is taking place in a cold climate. In these conditions, the quality of public-policy decisions becomes very important. Priority-setting and value-for-money considerations come to the fore. And at the forefront, government might wish to promote, according to Vani Borooah, growth with development. The talents and aptitude of each member of society should be given every chance to grow to their full potential and be appropriately rewarded.

Thus public policy should be concerned with more than maximising the growth of the economy as measured by GDP. Attention should be devoted to:
- reducing unemployment,
- eliminating educational underachievement,
- abolishing poverty,
- securing equality of opportunity, and
- mitigating inequality of income.

One of the important lessons of a recent study of successful European regions[6] is that the social dimension is crucial if a region is to be considered a success. ■

**Footnotes**

[1] This is the author's interpretation of the views expressed by the participants at the

seminar and it does not necessarily reflect those of the NIEC. I should like to thank colleagues at the council, Democratic Dialogue and the Eastern Health and Social Services Board for comments on an earlier draft.
[2] *Financial Times*, August 28th 1998
[3] S Smith, 'Regional government, fiscal and financial management in Northern Ireland', in Northern Ireland Economic Council, *Decentralised Government and Economic Performance in Northern Ireland*, occasional paper 7, NIEC, Belfast, 1996
[4] ibid
[5] P Bew, '100 days of Trimble and Mallon', *Belfast Telegraph*, October 7th 1998
[6] M Dunford and R Hudson, *Successful European Regions: Northern Ireland Learning from Others*, research monograph 3, NIEC, Belfast, 1996

# Notes on contributors

**Robin Wilson** is director of Democratic Dialogue.

**John Loughlin** is professor of European politics, and Jean Monnet chair in European political economy, at Cardiff University.

**Vani Borooah** is professor of applied economics at the University of Ulster.

**Richard Barnett** is professor of public finance and management, and dean of the faculty of business and management, at the University of Ulster.

**Graeme Hutchinson** recently completed his doctorate at the University of Ulster on the growth and impact of public expenditure in Northern Ireland.

**David Heald** is professor of accountancy at the University of Aberdeen and specialist adviser on public expenditure and government accounting to the Treasury Committee.

**Paul Gorecki** is director of the Northern Ireland Economic Council.

# DD publications

Reports are £7.50stg each for individuals, £10 for institutions, £4 for unwaged/students; please add 10 per cent p&p. Any six reports can be ordered for £37.50 net. Papers are £1 each, plus p&p. Orders can be by letter, phone, fax or e-mail; cheques are payable to Democratic Dialogue. Further details of the publications are on the DD web site.

## Reports

*Report 1:    New Thinking for New Times*
Report of DD's launch conference in Belfast in 1995, including keynote address on 'the new context of politics' by Prof Anthony Giddens, director of the London School of Economics (June 1995)

*Report 2:    Social Exclusion, Social Inclusion*
An international review of strategies to combat social exclusion, followed by concrete policy proposals to achieve a cohesive society in Northern Ireland (November 1995)

*Report 3:    Reconstituting Politics*
Radical new approaches to constitutional possibilities for Northern Ireland, citizen involvement in policy-making and the reinvention of politics itself (March 1996)

*Report 4:    Power, Politics, Positionings—Women in Northern Ireland*
An assessment of where women stand in the political parties, the voluntary sector and the media, and how their participation in public life can be enhanced (October 1996)

*Report 5:    Continentally Challenged—Securing Northern Ireland's Place in the
            European Union*
How Northern Ireland can reposition itself regionally in Europe, and articulate a more cohesive voice, against a fast-moving backdrop of change across the continent (February 1997)

*Report 6:    Politics—The Next Generation*
An unprecedented survey of the attitudes of young people, based on questionnaires and focus

groups, backing a case for political education and local youth representation (April 1997)

*Report 7:   With All Due Respect—Pluralism and Parity of Esteem*
Setting Northern Ireland's nationalism debate in the wider context of identity politics, and indicating how 'parity of esteem' can promote pluralism rather than polarisation (June 1997)

*Report 8:   Politics in Public—Freedom of Assembly and the Right to Protest*
A detailed comparative study demonstrating how the 'right to march' is qualified in diverse jurisdictions, pointing to a resolution of Northern Ireland's parades controversy (March 1998)

*Report 9:   New Order—International Models of Peace and Reconciliation*
An assessment of the Belfast agreement in the light of the evolving architecture for security and human rights in Europe, with a focus on non- and inter-governmental organisations (May 1998)

## Papers

*Media and Intrastate Conflict in Northern Ireland*
A paper commissioned by the European Institute for the Media (July 1997)

*Making 'consent' mutual*
An exploration of the 'consent principle' in Northern Ireland (October 1997)

*Making democracy work*
A paper commissioned by the Northern Ireland Council for Voluntary Action (February 1998)

*Economic governance—international experiences: a new direction for Northern Ireland*
A paper commissioned by the Confederation of British Industry Northern Ireland (March 1998)

*Two-tier policing—a middle way for Northern Ireland?*
An international model which could offer a way beyond a polarised debate (March 1998)

*Elections in Northern Ireland—systems for stability and success*
A look at options for elections to the Assembly to assist a gender balance (April 1998)

*Irish nationalisms in perspective*
Torkel Opsahl memorial lecture by Prof Fred Halliday of LSE (May 1998)

*The Civic Forum—a consultation document from New Agenda*
A discussion, derived from a civil society network, of the role of the Civic Forum (August 1998)

*Reinventing government—a once-only opportunity*
Proposals for holistic government and a departmental shake-up (August 1998)

*Scotland's parliament—lessons for Northern Ireland*
A cautionary story of the devolution debate in Scotland (September 1998)

# Recent NIEC publications

## Reports

104  *Northern Ireland and the Recent Recession: Cyclical Strength or Structural Weakness?* (August 1993)

105  Annual Report 1992-93 (October 1993)

106  Autumn Economic Review (October 1993)

107  *Transport Infrastructure and Policy in Northern Ireland* (November 1993)

108  Economic Assessment: April 1994

109  *The Impact of CAP Reform on Northern Ireland* (June 1994)

110  *The Reform of Health and Social Care in Northern Ireland: An Introduction to the Economic Issues* (July 1994)

111  *The Implications of Peripherality for Northern Ireland* (August 1994)

112  Annual Report 1993-94 (October 1994)

113  Autumn Economic Review (October 1994)

114  Annual Sir Charles Carter Lecture, 'Britain and Northern Ireland, The State We're In—Failure and Opportunity', by Will Hutton, economics editor of the *Guardian* (November 1994)

115  Annual Sir Charles Carter Lecture, 'Competitive Dynamics and Industrial Modernisation Programmes: Lessons from Japan and America', by Michael H Best, Centre for Industrial Competitiveness, University of Massachusetts, Lowell (September 1995)

116  Annual Report 1994-95 (October 1995)

117  *Taxes, Benefits, Unemployment and Poverty Traps in Northern Ireland* (November 1995)

118  *The 1995 UK Budget: Background and Implications for Northern Ireland* (February 1996)

119  Annual Report 1995-96 (Oct 1996)

120  Annual Sir Charles Carter Lecture, 'Reforming Education in the United Kingdom: The Vital Priorities', by Sir Claus Moser KCB CBE FBA, The British Museum Development Trust (January 1997)

121  *Rising to the Challenge: The Future of Tourism in Northern Ireland* (February 1997)

122  *The 1996 UK Budget: Implications for Northern Ireland* (March 1997)

123  *Industrial Policy Assessment and Performance Measurement—The Case of the IDB* (April 1997)

124  Annual Report 1996-97 (October 1997)

125  *The 1997 UK Budget: Implications for Northern Ireland* (November 1997)

126  Annual Sir Charles Carter Lecture, 'Setting Priorities for Health Care: Why Government Should Take the Lead', by Chris Ham, Professor of Health Policy and Management and Director, Health Services Management Centre, University of Birmingham (January 1998)

127  *A Framework for Economic Development: The Implications for Northern Ireland of the 1998 UK and EU Budgets and the Chancellor's Economic Strategy for Northern Ireland* (June 1998)

## Occasional paper series

1  *Reforming the Educational System in Northern Ireland: A Comment on 'Learning for Life' and Recent Developments in the Education System* (January 1995)

2  *Demographic Trends in Northern Ireland: Key Findings and Policy Implications* (March 1995)

3  'Through Peace to Prosperity', proceedings of the peace seminar hosted by the Economic Council (April 1995)

4  *The Economic Implications of Peace and Political Stability for Northern Ireland* (June 1995). A supplementary paper to NIEC Occasional Paper 4: *The Implications of Peace and Political Stability in Northern Ireland for Selected Sectors: Inward Investment, Tourism*

*and Security* (June 1995)

5  *Health and Personal Social Services to the Millennium: A Response to* **Regional Strategy for Health and Social Wellbeing, 1997-2002** (December 1995)

6  *Building A Better Future: A Response to* **Building on Success. Proposals for Future Housing Policy** (May 1996)

7  'Decentralised Government and Economic Performance in Northern Ireland', proceedings of the seminar sponsored by the NIEC in association with the University of Ulster on 19 June 1996 at the University of Ulster at Jordanstown (December 1996)

8  *Towards Resolving Long-Term Unemployment in Northern Ireland. A Response to the* **Long-Term Unemployment Consultation Document** *(*June 1997)

9  *The Impact of a National Minimum Wage on the Northern Ireland Economy. A Response to the Low Pay Commission* (February 1998)

## Research monograph series

1  *Demographic Review Northern Ireland 1995*, by Paul Compton (March 1995)

2  *The Arts and the Northern Ireland Economy*, by John Myerscough with a statement by the Economic Council (January 1996)

3  *Successful European Regions: Northern Ireland Learning From Others*, by Michael Dunford and Ray Hudson with a statement by the Economic Council (November 1996)

4  *Educational Achievement in Northern Ireland: Patterns and Prospects*, by Tony § Gallagher, Ian Shuttleworth and Colette Gray with a statement by the Economic Council (December 1997)

5  *Competitiveness and Industrial Policy in Northern Ireland*, by John H Dunning, Edward Bannerman and Sarianna M Lundan with a statement by the Economic Council (March 1998)

6  *Regional Economic and Policy Impacts of EMU: The Case of Northern Ireland*, edited by John Bradley with a statement by the Economic Council (April 1998)

7  *Improving Schools in Northern Ireland*, by Tony Gallagher, Ian Shuttleworth and Colette Gray with a statement by the Economic Council (August 1998)